Programming APIs with C# and .NET

Develop high-performance APIs that ensure seamless application communication and enhanced security

Jesse Liberty

Joseph Dluzen

Programming APIs with C# and .NET

Associate Group Product Manager: Kunal Sawant

Book Project Manager: Prajakta Naik

Publishing Product Manager: Srishti Seth

Book Coordinator: Manisha Singh

Senior Editor: Rounak Kulkarni

Technical Editor: Vidhisha Patidar

Copy Editor: Safis Editing

Indexer: Rekha Nair

Production Designer: Gokul Raj S.T

Business Development Executive: Sonia Chauhan

First published: November 2024

Production reference:1251024

Published by Packt Publishing Ltd.
Grosvenor House
11 St Paul's Square
Birmingham
B3 1RB, UK.

ISBN 978-1-83546-885-2

www.packtpub.com

To my 106-year-old mother, my wife, and especially my children. I am a very lucky man.

– Jesse Liberty

To my wife, children, and parents.

– Joseph Dluzen

Contributors

About the authors

Jesse Liberty specializes in C#, Git, and building world-class APIs. He hosts the popular *Yet Another Podcast* (`https://jesseliberty.com/podcast/`) and is the author of more than two dozen best-selling programming books (`https://packt.link/FVtEr`).

Jesse was a Technical Evangelist for Microsoft, Distinguished Software Engineer at AT&T; Software Architect for PBS, and Vice President of Information Technology at Citibank. He was also on the teaching staff at Brandeis University. Jesse has been a Microsoft MVP for 13 years.

Jesse is a recognized expert and has spoken at conferences worldwide. His website is `https://jesseliberty.com`.

I have so many people to thank, starting with my co-author, Joe Dluzen, without whom this book would literally have been impossible. I'd also like to thank all the people at Packt, especially Rounak, Prajakta, Kunal, and Vidhisha who stuck in there with us, as well as the technical reviewer. The quality of this book is due to their diligence, though any mistakes are ours. I'd also like to thank my boss for his encouragement and for teaching me so much about creating world-class enterprise APIs. Finally, as ever, I wish to thank my wife, without whose patience and encouragement I could never have written any of my books.

Joseph Dluzen has been working in C# and associated frameworks for almost 20 years. He is currently in a software architecture role for one of the world's largest agricultural machine manufacturers. Formerly a senior consultant at Accenture, he has experience in a wide range of industries, including government identity, autonomous vehicle tooling, and enterprise auction management systems.

I would like to thank Jesse, without whom this book would never have happened.

About the reviewer

Matheus de Campos , based out of Brazil, is a software engineer with a Bachelor's degree in Computer Science. He has extensive international experience and specializes in Microsoft technologies. Currently, he works as a consultant for tech organizations, focusing on delivering impactful solutions that optimize technology strategies.

Table of Contents

4

Documentation with Swagger 33

5

Data Validation 43

6

Azure Functions 53

10

Deploying to Azure   123

11

What's Next?   137

Index   141

Other Books You May Enjoy   146

Preface

Building a good **Application Program Interface (API)** is essential for creating real-world applications that display data from a data source (most often a database). The job of the API, as you'll see in this book, is the separation of concerns on a large scale; specifically separating the concerns of the frontend from the backend. This allows you to change one (e.g., swap out a new database) without breaking the other (e.g., a website) or vice versa.

A typical enterprise might have multiple teams working on the same overall product. For example, you might have a team working on a web presentation of your data, another working on the iOS version, and a third working on Android.

On the backend, you might have multiple data sources. In the simple example that we use in this book, we examine a car dealership. It might have input from sales, but also from inventory, from a service that provides information on average prices, and so forth. Some of this is static data easily stored in a database, some must be in a frequently updated cache, and some must be obtained on demand.

Coordinating the frontend with the backend is difficult and subject to catastrophic breakage should, for example, the format or calculations in the backend change. Furthermore, the needs of the presentation level are almost guaranteed to change over time. Finally, the frontend is most often not the ideal place to put your business logic.

APIs solve these problems. The frontend talks to well-defined endpoints, and the backend responds with well-defined data. What the backend does to get and manipulate that data is invisible to the frontend. For that matter, the uses that the frontend puts that data to are invisible to the backend. Most importantly, the API itself doesn't need to know about either; it just knows what is being asked for and how to get it.

Who this book is for

This book is targeted at programmers with at least a working knowledge of C# who want to create world-class APIs, often for enterprise applications. It assumes no prior experience with APIs, though a working acquaintance with SQL will be helpful.

What this book covers

Chapter 1, Getting Started, provides a quick start to get everything set up locally for development.

Chapter 2, What We'll Build, provides an overview of an API in general, and how to use it to decouple a frontend and backend system.

Chapter 3, Implementing with REST, provides an overview of best practices and an opinionated design for general API development that is used throughout the industry.

Chapter 4, Documentation with Swagger, shows you how to enable and surface documentation based on Swagger.

Chapter 5, Data Validation, provides an overview of how to validate API calls, including custom validation with a widely used library.

Chapter 6, Azure Functions, provides an alternative cloud-first hosting framework that not only can be used for APIs but also as a starting point for much more. It also illustrates best practices and then builds upon them to allow runtime configuration without redeployment.

Chapter 7, Azure Durable Functions, provides an overview of the simplification that results when following a few small design rules in a stateful, scalable system.

Chapter 8, Advanced Topics, provides a straightforward, cost-effective, cloud logging implementation. Additionally, it goes over advanced scenarios such as complex object mapping, an opinionated cloud-first design tool, and the creation and use of storage tables.

Chapter 9, Authentication and Authorization, provides an out-of-the-box solution for cloud-first authentication scenarios, including authorizing Azure and non-Azure clients.

Chapter 10, Deploying to Azure, gets you set up quickly to iterate with **Continuous Delivery and Continuous Integration (CI/CD)** pipelines.

Chapter 11, What's Next?, gives you practical advice on the classic question: Now what?

To get the most out of this book

You will need a working knowledge of at least the basics of C#. An acquaintance with SQL is helpful but not required. The use of Git and repositories in general will make your life easier. We assume no other technical expertise.

Software/hardware covered in the book (no additional knowledge expected other than as above)	Operating system/Other requirements
PC	Windows
Intermediate C#	Windows
Swagger	Windows
Basic DevOps	Azure
AutoMapper	Windows
SQL Server or equivalent	Windows
Git	GitHub

All the setup necessary to follow along with this book is explained as we go.

If you are using the digital version of this book, we advise you to type the code yourself or access the code from the book's GitHub repository (a link is available in the next section). Doing so will help you avoid any potential errors related to the copying and pasting of code.

Writing the code yourself has been proven to be a more effective way to learn new material.

Download the example code files

You can download the example code files for this book from GitHub at `https://github.com/PacktPublishing/Programming-APIs-with-C-Sharp-and-.NET`. If there's an update to the code, it will be updated in the GitHub repository.

We also have other code bundles from our rich catalog of books and videos available at `https://github.com/PacktPublishing/`. Check them out!

Conventions used

There are a number of text conventions used throughout this book.

`Code in text`: Indicates code words in text, database table names, folder names, filenames, file extensions, pathnames, dummy URLs, and user input. Here is an example: "This can be changed in the `host.json` file under the `extensions > http > routePrefix` setting:"

A block of code is set as follows:

```
{
  "version": "2.0",
  "logging": {
    "applicationInsights": {
      "samplingSettings": {
        "isEnabled": true,
        "excludedTypes": "Request"
      },
      "enableLiveMetricsFilters": true
    }
  },
  "extensions": {
    "http": {
      "routePrefix": "myapi"
    }
  }
}
```

When we wish to draw your attention to a particular part of a code block, the relevant lines or items are set in bold:

```
CarDtoValidator validator = new CarDtoValidator();
var result = validator.Validate(carAsDto);
if (!result.IsValid)
{
    return BadRequest(result.Errors);
}
```

Any command-line input or output is written as follows:

```
git clone https://github.com/MicrosoftDocs/mslearn-dotnet-cloudnative-
devops.git eShopLite
```

Bold: Indicates a new term, an important word, or words that you see onscreen. For instance, words in menus or dialog boxes appear in **bold**. Here is an example: "Select **Azure Function App (Linux)** and click **Next**."

> **Tips or important notes**
> Appear like this.

Get in touch

Feedback from our readers is always welcome.

General feedback: If you have questions about any aspect of this book, email us at customercare@ packtpub.com and mention the book title in the subject of your message.

Errata: Although we have taken every care to ensure the accuracy of our content, mistakes do happen. If you have found a mistake in this book, we would be grateful if you would report this to us. Please visit www.packtpub.com/support/errata and fill in the form.

Piracy: If you come across any illegal copies of our works in any form on the internet, we would be grateful if you would provide us with the location address or website name. Please contact us at copyright@packt.com with a link to the material.

If you are interested in becoming an author: If there is a topic that you have expertise in and you are interested in either writing or contributing to a book, please visit authors.packtpub.com.

Share Your Thoughts

Once you've read *Programming APIs with C# and .NET*, we'd love to hear your thoughts! Scan the QR code below to go straight to the Amazon review page for this book and share your feedback.

https://packt.link/r/1835468853

Your review is important to us and the tech community and will help us make sure we're delivering excellent quality content.

Download a free PDF copy of this book

Thanks for purchasing this book!

Do you like to read on the go but are unable to carry your print books everywhere?

Is your eBook purchase not compatible with the device of your choice?

Don't worry, now with every Packt book you get a DRM-free PDF version of that book at no cost.

Read anywhere, any place, on any device. Search, copy, and paste code from your favorite technical books directly into your application.

The perks don't stop there, you can get exclusive access to discounts, newsletters, and great free content in your inbox daily

Follow these simple steps to get the benefits:

1. Scan the QR code or visit the link below

https://packt.link/free-ebook/978-1-83546-885-2

2. Submit your proof of purchase
3. That's it! We'll send your free PDF and other benefits to your email directly

1

Getting Started

Let's start by making sure you're in the right place. This is a book about creating **Application Programming Interfaces** (**APIs**) using .NET. Along the way, we will look at a very simple backend (database) and frontend (user interface) and the tools we use to create and test APIs.

The core responsibility of an API is to decouple an application (web, mobile, and so on) from the backend (database, another API, and more). The API sits between the frontend (the user interface to your application) and the backend (for our purposes, a database).

In this chapter, we're going to cover the following main topics:

- What software you will need
- How to obtain the software you need
- Installing Visual Studio

Technical requirements

To proceed through this book, you will need a computer running Windows (10 or 11) and an internet connection. It is best if your computer has at least 16 GB of memory, and, of course, you'll need room on your disk for the software and for the code you will write.

You can create APIs on any platform (e.g., Linux) and use any development environment (e.g., Visual Studio Code instead of Visual Studio). This book, however, will focus on Visual Studio and Windows as they are the most popular and arguably the most powerful way to create .NET APIs.

The code files for this book are available in the book's GitHub repository: `https://github.com/PacktPublishing/Programming-APIs-with-C-Sharp-and-.NET`.

Where does the API fit in?

When you are creating a decoupled application, your principal parts are:

- The front end
- The back end
- The middleware

A typical front end might be a web application, a mobile application, or other ways of displaying data.

A typical backend might be a database or another service.

The middleware sits between the front end and the back end. The most important middleware is the API. The job of the API is to ensure that the front end and back end are decoupled – that is, you can modify one without affecting the other. This is simply good programming practice and will save you hours (or months) of rewriting should either of these change (which they will!).

The players

Typically, the backend and the frontend are created by different teams, though, of course, you can have one developer creating it all. We're also going to restrict our backend to a simple database, though any source of data can be a backend. Finally, we're not going to build a full frontend (that would be a distraction from the point of this book) but, rather, we're going to use a tool, **Postman**, to mimic a frontend. There will be more on Postman throughout this book.

Getting set up

You can create your backend, API, and frontend on any operating system you like. For this book, we'll be creating all three on Windows, using **Visual Studio 2022**, the latest Postman, and **Dapper** as a simple **Object Relational Mapper** (**ORM**) to make our lives easier. There are a few other simple tools we'll be using, so let's get you set up.

Downloading the free software you need

To get started, if you don't have Visual Studio installed, go to `https://visualstudio.com` and click on **Downloads** (this site changes frequently but the basic steps remain the same). You have three choices of which version to download: **Community**, **Professional**, and **Enterprise**. The Community version is free and will provide all you need to follow along in this book.

When you click on your choice, Visual Studio Setup will download to your `downloads` directory. Double-click on it and click on **Yes** at the security prompt. The installer will update itself and then will begin the installation. This can take a little while, but don't go away as you have some selections to make.

> **Note**
>
> If you have Visual Studio installed but for some reason want to install the Community Edition as well, that is no problem as they can run side by side.

A menu will appear similar to *Figure 1.1* (if it does not, click **Modify**).

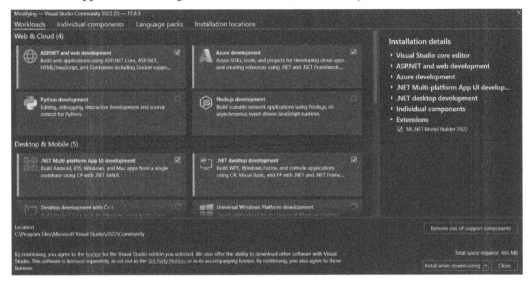

Figure 1.1 – Setting up Visual Studio: please note that this screenshot
intends to show the layout, so text readability is not essential

Be sure that **ASP.NET and web development** is checked. Scroll down and check **Data storage and processing** (if you are short on disk space, skip this one). Once you are satisfied, click on **Install while downloading** and then click on **Modify**.

SQL Server will be installed for you, as will **SQL Server Management Studio** (**SSMS**). You will typically interact with SQL Server through SSMS. We will look at how to work with this tool, and all the others, as we go.

Your next tool is Dapper. This is a small, lightweight ORM (often called a micro-ORM) that does one important part of the work of the much bigger SQL platform, Entity Framework, but with much less overhead. Specifically, Dapper will map queries to objects.

Since our needs will be minimal, Dapper will be more than enough. You can read more about Dapper here: `https://www.learndapper.com/`.

We will mimic our user interface with Postman, which we will also use for end-to-end testing. You can get the latest version of Postman at `https://postman.com/downloads`. You can also access Postman through your browser, but we'll be using the downloaded version.

Postman is surprisingly powerful, and we will review how we will use it as we go along. That said, we will only scratch the surface of what you can do with this tool, so at some point, you may want to read the documentation.

We will be using Swagger for documentation (see *Chapter 4*), and the built-in logger functionality for (surprise!) logging errors and issues that will not be surfaced to the user, but which will be useful for you as the programmer.

Summary

In this chapter, you saw what software you will need, how to download it, and how to install it. All of the software we'll be using in this book is free. In the next chapter, we will see the example application that we'll build to illustrate a meaningful use of an API.

You try it

Be sure to download and install all of the software described if you want to follow along as we create the API.

2
What We'll Build

In this chapter, we will provide a context for the rest of the book. That context is a simple application for buying and selling cars. We will not build out this application but, in fact, we'll have only one type of object (`Car`) and one table in our database. This will allow us to focus on the API rather than getting hung up on database design.

In this chapter, we're going to cover the following main topics:

- What an API is and what it is for
- The backend database that we will use throughout the book
- The application that we will build throughout the book
- The `Car` object that we will use to demonstrate CRUD operations

We will use only free software, as shown in the *Technical requirements* section, and we will take advantage of open source utilities such as Dapper and AutoMapper, both introduced in *Chapter 1*.

Technical requirements

For this chapter, you'll need **Visual Studio** and **SQL Server Management Studio (SSMS)**, as well as **Postman**. Remember that SSMS was installed with Visual Studio.

Note that you can also manage your database from within Visual Studio using the Server Explorer and the SQL Server Object Explorer.

The code files for this book are available in the book's GitHub repository: `https://github.com/PacktPublishing/Programming-APIs-with-C-Sharp-and-.NET/tree/main/Chapter02`

What is an API and what is it for?

The purpose of an API is to decouple the backend of an application (e.g., a database) from the frontend (e.g., a web application or mobile application), as illustrated in *Figure 2.1*.

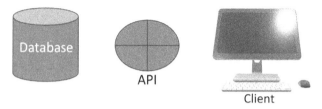

Figure 2.1 – Separation of concerns

The client does not talk directly to the database but rather talks to the API, which, in turn, talks to the database. The huge advantage of this approach is that you can modify the database and the client does not have to change. Alternatively, you can modify the front end (for example, a website) without changing the database.

These modifications take place throughout the development of a large project and continue after delivery. It is imperative, especially with a mobile application, that you can modify the backend without forcing the user to update the application. Even with web applications, however, this can be critical, as the team maintaining the database may well not be the team maintaining the client.

Creating the database

To illustrate all the aspects of an API, we will create an incredibly simple database and we'll use Postman to stand in for our client. Postman lets you call into the API and see what the client would get back. Actually, it can do a lot more, but that is the principal way we'll use it.

We'll keep both the backend and the frontend as simple as we can so that we can focus on the API.

The application

The database we'll be creating will be used in a simple (fictional) application for buying and selling cars. The database will keep a list of automobiles along with details of their engine, performance, and so on. A short example of this data is shown in *Figure 2.2*.

	name	mpg	cylinders	displacement	horsepower	weight	acceleration	model_year	origin	is_deleted	id
1	chevrolet chevelle malibu	18	8	307	130	3504	12	70	usa	0	1
2	buick skylark 320	15	8	350	165	3693	11.5	70	usa	0	2
3	plymouth satellite	18	8	318	150	3436	11	70	usa	1	3
4	subaru impreza	16	8	304	150	3433	12	22	usa	0	4
5	subaru impreza	17	8	302	140	3449	10.5	22	Korea	0	5
6	ford galaxie 500	15	8	429	198	4341	10	70	usa	0	6
7	chevrolet impala	14	8	454	220	4354	9	70	usa	0	7

Figure 2.2 – A subset of the data table we'll be using

Creating the Car Table

The data for the Car table is from the free *Automobile* dataset at https://kaggle.com. Download the data and import it into a database named Cars and a table named Car. The columns should take care of themselves.

The datasets on Kaggle change frequently, so your list of cars may look a bit different. All the datasets are all presented as .csv files, so just download one and open **SSMS** in order to do the import. Here are the steps:

1. Log into SSMS and create a database.

2. Create a table named CARS.

3. Start the **Import Data Wizard**. To do so, right-click on the table, and from the context menu select **Import Data**.

4. The **Choose a Data Source** dialog will appear. Select **Flat File Source** and click on **Browse** to find and select the CSV you got from Kaggle.

5. You will be asked for the destination. Choose **SQL Server Native Client**.

6. Review your settings and click **Save**.

After you complete the import, you will need to add two columns: is_deleted (initialize all rows to 0) and id, which should be your primary key and which should increment automatically.

We're ready to write a small application that will support the basic CRUD operations against our shiny new database.

If you run into a crisis and can't get it to work, try one of the following two options to get you up and running fast:

1. Go to stackoverflow.com and look for importing csv into flat database or

2. Grab the code from the *Chapter 3* folder of this book's repository, which will have the database already set up

The problem with the second alternative is that you'll have code we won't yet have explained. But not to worry, if you follow the steps above all should be fine. ("*Open the pod bay doors Hal.*")

> **Note**
> **CRUD** is an acronym for **Create, Read, Update, and Delete**. That is, create new records, read the records that match criteria, update records, and mark records as deleted.

Database structure

Our database consists of just one table: `Car`. As shown in *Figure 2.2*, that table must store various attributes of each car (name, miles per gallon, number of cylinders, and so on). *Figure 2.3* shows the table:

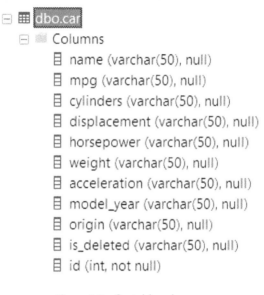

Figure 2.3 – Car table columns

Notice the `is_deleted` column. We'll be using "soft delete" – that is, rather than removing a row on deletion we'll just set `is_deleted` to true (`1`). That allows us to easily restore that column just by changing that value back to `0` (false).

Other than `id`, all of the columns are strings, which will make working with them easier.

Car object

Corresponding to the `Car` table, our code has a `Car` entity (`Cars/Data/Entities/Car.cs`):

```
namespace Cars.Data.Entities;
public class Car
{
    public int Id { get; set; }
    public string name { get; set; } = null!;
    public string mpg { get; set; } = null!;
    public string cylinders { get; set; } = null!;
    public string displacement { get; set; } = null!;
    public string horsepower { get; set; } = null!;
    public string weight { get; set; } = null!;
```

```
    public string acceleration { get; set; } = null!;
    public string model_year { get; set; } = null!;
    public string origin { get; set; } = null!;
    public string? is_deleted { get; set;}
}
```

We won't bother with **Data Transfer Objects** (**DTOs**) in this example, if only to keep things simple, though we will use them later in the book.

The ASP.NET application

To get started, create a new ASP.NET project using the ASP.NET Core Web API template. Put the files wherever is convenient for you and choose the latest version of .NET (this book was written with .NET 8).

The basic structure of our application will be as follows:

- Controllers with endpoints

- Services

- Repositories

We'll review endpoints and all the rest of this as we go.

Program.cs

You won't have to edit `Program.cs` for this application but it is worth a few minutes of your time to review it:

```
using Cars.Data;
using Cars.Data.Interfaces;
using Cars.Data.Repositories;

var builder = WebApplication.CreateBuilder(args);

// Add services to the container.
builder.Services.AddControllers();

// Learn more about configuring Swagger/OpenAPI at https://aka.ms/
aspnetcore/swashbuckle
builder.Services.AddEndpointsApiExplorer();
builder.Services.AddSwaggerGen();

// Load DB configuration and register the connection factory for
//injection
```

```
var configuration = builder.Configuration;
builder.Services.Configure<DbSettings>(configuration.
GetSection("ConnectionStrings"));
builder.Services.AddTransient<DatabaseConnectionFactory>();
builder.Services.AddTransient<CarRepository>();
builder.Services.RegisterDataAccessDependencies();

var app = builder.Build();

// Configure the HTTP request pipeline.
if (app.Environment.IsDevelopment())
{
    app.UseSwagger();
    app.UseSwaggerUI();
}

app.UseHttpsRedirection();

app.UseAuthorization();

app.MapControllers();

app.Run();
```

One thing to notice right away is the references to Swagger. We'll be using Swagger to automatically generate documentation for our project, as you'll see as we go.

Connecting to the database

The out-of-the-box project cannot know how to connect to your database. This information is contained in appsettings.json and in appsettings.Development.json (to get to the latter, expand the former).

appsettings.json is pretty simple:

```
{
  "Logging": {
    "LogLevel": {
      "Default": "Information",
      "Microsoft.AspNetCore": "Warning"
    }
  },
  "ConnectionStrings": {
    "DefaultConnection": "Data Source=localhost;Initial
```

```
      Catalog=Cars;Integrated Security=true"
   },
   "AllowedHosts": "*"
}
```

The key here is the `DefaultConnection` string, which sets up using the `Cars` database in the localhost.

The actual connection string is in `appsettings.Development.json`:

```
{
   "Logging": {
     "LogLevel": {
       "Default": "Information",
       "Microsoft.AspNetCore": "Warning"
     }
   },
   "ConnectionStrings": {
       "DefaultConnection": "Server=(localdb)\\
       mssqllocaldb;Database=Cars;Trusted_
       Connection=True;MultipleActiveResultSets=true"
   }
}
```

The two other files you'll need to complete this connection are `DatabaseConnectionFactory` and `DbSettings`. These are provided for you.

The following refers to objects in `DbSettings.cs`:

```
namespace Cars.Data;

public class DbSettings
{
    public string DefaultConnection { get; set; } = null!; // https://
    learn.microsoft.com/en-us/dotnet/csharp/language-reference/
    compiler-messages/nullable-warnings#nonnullable-reference-not-
    initialized
}
```

Finally, under `Properties`, you'll find the `launchsettings.json` file:

```
{
   "$schema": "https://json.schemastore.org/launchsettings.json",
   "iisSettings": {
     "windowsAuthentication": false,
```

```json
      "anonymousAuthentication": true,
      "iisExpress": {
        "applicationUrl": "http://localhost:35187",
        "sslPort": 44306
      }
    },
    "profiles": {
      "http": {
        "commandName": "Project",
        "dotnetRunMessages": true,
        "launchBrowser": true,
        "launchUrl": "swagger",
        "applicationUrl": "http://localhost:5283",
        "environmentVariables": {
          "ASPNETCORE_ENVIRONMENT": "Development"
        }
      },
      "https": {
        "commandName": "Project",
        "dotnetRunMessages": true,
        "launchBrowser": true,
        "launchUrl": "swagger",
        "applicationUrl": "https://localhost:7025;http://
        localhost:5283",
        "environmentVariables": {
          "ASPNETCORE_ENVIRONMENT": "Development"
        }
      },
      "IIS Express": {
        "commandName": "IISExpress",
        "launchBrowser": true,
        "launchUrl": "swagger",
        "environmentVariables": {
          "ASPNETCORE_ENVIRONMENT": "Development"
        }
      }
    }
  }
}
```

All of this is worth a look but don't fret about it; almost all of it is supplied for you, and all of it is in the sample code in our repository.

Folders

To organize our application, we will create the following folders:

- `Controllers`
- `Data`
- `Interfaces`
- `Repositories`
- `Services`

Let's briefly explain what these are:

- The *client* is the application calling the API (for example, the website or mobile application). The `Controllers` folder will hold methods that act as *endpoints* (an endpoint is what the client connects to via a URL).
- The `Data` folder will hold the definition of our *entities* – in our case, the `Car` object shown earlier.
- The `Interfaces` folder is just what it sounds like: it will hold the interfaces to our C# objects.
- The `Repositories` folder will hold the code between our methods and the database calls.
- The `Services` folder will hold supporting code.

The flow will be as follows:

1. The client calls a method in a controller.
2. The method calls a service to handle the business logic.
3. The service calls a method in the repository, which, in turn, calls into the database.

Again, we'll examine the details as we go, starting in the next chapter.

Summary

In this chapter, you saw what an API is and how it is used to separate the front end (e.g., a web site) from the backend (e.g., a database). We also looked at the simple database and application that we'll use throughout the book.

In order to demonstrate CRUD operations, we'll build a simple application focused on a `Car` object as if we were working with an inventory of cars. We imported it from `https://kaggle.com`.

This lays the groundwork for the rest of the chapters and for the simple application that we will build. Our focus will be strictly on creating APIs, so we will spend little time on database technology or even on the frontend.

You try it

This is a good time to create your application and the database. If you are adventurous, create a similar but different application, database, and data entity. This will ensure that you cement the elements we'll be using.

3

Implementing with REST

In the previous chapter, we created a simple database and object (`Car`) to interact with. In this chapter, we'll look at the **Representation State Transfer** (**REST**) protocol and how it is used in APIs. REST is the most popular protocol for creating APIs.

We will see how REST contributes to creating a client/server architecture, and with it, desirable separation of concerns. We will cover the following topics in this chapter:

- Understanding what REST is
- Looking at standard web protocols
- The first implementation of a REST API
- What **Data Transfer Objects** (**DTOs**) are and how to use them
- Using Postman as our frontend

By the time you finish this chapter, you will understand the fundamentals of creating simple APIs.

Technical requirements

For this chapter, you will need **Visual Studio**, **AutoMapper**, and **Dapper**. Please see *Chapter 1, Getting Started*, for how to obtain these. The code files for this chapter can be found in the GitHub repository here: `https://github.com/PacktPublishing/Programming-APIs-with-C-Sharp-and-.NET/tree/main/Chapter03`

REST

One of the key concepts in REST is the separation of concerns. This idea will be familiar to you as a C# programmer. Here, we are separating the concerns of the server and the client.

The API can only respond to calls from the client, and cannot generate calls of its own. Note that within the logic of the API implementation, it is possible to call other APIs, but not back to the client.

The server is in no way dependent on the design or implementation of the client.

Client/server

The key to a REST application is that the API can be called by any type of client: web application, phone application, and so on. Further, the client can be located anywhere and there are no constraints on the architecture of the client.

The same is true for the backend, behind the API. Typically, this will be a database, but it can be any type of data storage: relational, object, in memory, and so on.

One way to accomplish this, is to use the standard web protocols such as GET, PUT, and so forth. This approach is essential to REST. In fact, for many people this is the virtual definition of REST.

Using web protocols

In REST, we use the same verbs as we do in HTTP: GET, PUT, POST, and DELETE. In addition, the API returns standard web values to the client, for example, 404 (not found), 200 (success), 201 (created), and so on.

Each request from the client to the API will consist of an HTTP header, body, and meta-data. The client expresses which API is wanted by calling a URL, and passes needed data (e.g., the id value for the requested entity either in the URL or, if passing too much data for a URL, in the body of the request. For example, here is a POST to add a car to the backend database. Don't worry about the syntax for now; rather, take a look at the URL and the body of the request in *Figure 3.1*.

Figure 3.1 – Sending data for insertion

At the top of the figure, we see the URL (`https://localhost:7025/Car`). This is the "address" of the API. Notice that the last part of the URL is *Car*. This is the name of the controller.

Below the URL is a menu allowing you to see the parameters being sent, the Authorization any headers that go along as meta-data (see *Figure 3.2*), the body that we see in *Figure 3.1*, any scripts to run before sending the request, tests to ensure we are getting back the right data (see *Chapter 8, Advanced Topics*), and any settings we need for the request.

The numbered lines 1-12 in the preceding figure are the body of this request. We are inserting a car into the database and so all the data for the insertion is here in JSON format. Notice that there is no ID; that will be assigned on the backend.

Figure 3.2 – Headers

These headers provide vital information to the server. They must be sent for each interaction because REST is inherently stateless.

Statelessness and caching

REST APIs are stateless, so you must treat each call to the API as independent from all other calls.

Note that if you need state and you are on Azure, you'll want a durable function, which is covered in *Chapter 7, Azure Durable Functions*.

While you cannot maintain state between calls, the server can cache data for faster retrieval. This can significantly improve performance There are a number of platforms that can support REST APIs; the one we will focus on for this book, and the platform of choice for .NET, is ASP.NET Core.

An alternative to REST is GraphQL. There are two problems this designed to solve: overfetching and underfetching. The user wants to send a single API call to the server. In order to do this, they must designate what data is needed. If a Car entity is requested, it may be that they don't care at all about some of the features of the car but they get the entire car as part of the API. This is called overfetching. On the other hand, if they designate an API that only gets the type of car, this may be under fetching (they have to make a second call for the rest of what they need). GraphQL is designed to solve this problem, allowing the client to specify exactly which properties are requested.

That said, the downside of GraphQL is that each API query must be hand-crafted to designate what is wanted.

Because of this, and other technical constraints, not the least of which is inertia, REST is by far the most popular way to write APIs and we will not cover GraphQL in this book.

Implementing REST in ASP.NET Core

An API created in ASP.NET Core will typically have three major components:

- Controllers
- Services
- Repositories

> **Note**
> There is an alternative to controller-based APIs known as Minimal APIs. We discuss this in brief towards the end of this chapter (refer to the *Minimal APIs* box). We do not cover Minimal APIs for the rest of the book as they have too many limitations.

When you invoke an API with a URL, that address is resolved to a controller. For example, using the URL we saw earlier, if you call `https://localhost:7025/Car`, you will invoke the `CarController` at that address. Note that ASP.NET uses "convention over configuration," by which we mean that *by convention*, the part of the word Controller is left off the address but is implied. So in this case, `CarController`, the address just uses `Car` (leaving off Controller).

The job of the controller is to ensure that the user has been authenticated (it's really them) and authorized (they have permission to take whatever action is invoked). The controller then assembles any needed data and passes it along to the Service. Typically, but not necessarily, this will be called `CarService` and will sit in a folder with other services.

The job of the Service is to handle any business logic and prepare the data to go into the database. It then passes the data to the repository.

Similar to the Service, the repository would typically be called `CarRepository` and would be located in a folder along with other repositories. The job of the repository is to interact with the underlying data storage (for example, a database).

Often, you will want to separate the properties of the database from the properties of an object to be sent through the API. For that, we use DTOs.

DTOs

It is common to use DTOs to separate the representation of the structure of the database from a supporting **Plain Old C# Object (POCO)**

Let's take an example from a relational database. Each row may have twelve columns but for a specific API request, only seven are needed. The DTO will be a class with seven properties, and we'll use a tool (`AutoMapper`) to map the values in the seven columns to the seven properties.

Installing AutoMapper

The easiest way to install `AutoMapper` is to download the NuGet packages, as shown in *Figure 3.3*:

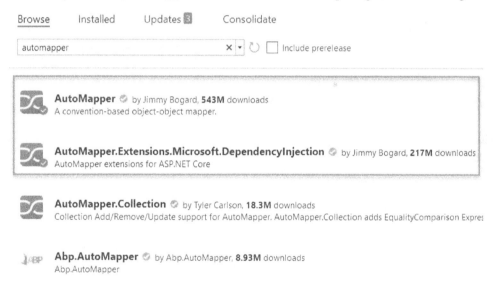

Figure 3.3 – Installing AutoMapper

There is a bit of configuration for `AutoMapper`, but it is only done once. In `Program.cs`, add the following:

```
builder.Services.AddAutoMapper(typeof(Program));
```

The next step is to create the DTO class itself.

Creating the DTO class

The POCO classes we've created directly track the columns in the database, as described earlier. The DTO class tracks some or all of these columns as properties:

```
namespace Cars.Data.DTOs
{
    public class CarDto
    {
        public int Id { get; set; }
        public string Name { get; set; }
        public string Mpg { get; set; }
        public string Cylinders { get; set; }
        public string Displacement { get; set; }
        public string Horsepower { get; set; }
        public string Weight { get; set; }
        public string Acceleration { get; set; }
        public string ModelYear { get; set; }
        public string Origin { get; set; }
    }
}
```

Once your DTO is in place, you need a way to map the properties in the DTO to the properties in the database (POCO) class. We can do that in a profile.

Setting up the profile

While we are here, let's set up the profile file for the `Car` entity. The `AutoMapper` tool (no pun intended) provides a base class, `Profile`, that we will derive from.

Create a file called `CarProfile.cs` and put this code in it:

```
Public class CarProfile : Profile
{
    Public CarProfile()
    {
        CreateMap<CarDto, Car>()
          .ForMember(car => car.id, opt=>opt.MapFrom(carDto => carDto.
          Id))
          .ForMember(car => car.name, opt=>opt.MapFrom(carDto => carDto.
          Name))
          .ForMember(car => car.mpg, opt=>opt.MapFrom(carDto => carDto.
          Mpg))
          .ForMember(car => car.cylinders, opt=>opt.MapFrom(carDto =>
          carDto.Cylinders))
          .ForMember(car => car.displacement, opt=>opt.MapFrom(carDto =>
```

```
carDto.Displacement))
.ForMember(car => car.horsepower, opt=>opt.MapFrom(carDto =>
carDto.Horsepower))
.ForMember(car => car.weight, opt=>opt.MapFrom(carDto =>
carDto.Weight))
.ForMember(car => car.acceleration, opt=>opt.MapFrom(carDto =>
carDto.Acceleration))
.ForMember(car => car.model_year, opt=>opt.MapFrom(carDto =>
carDto.ModelYear))
.ForMember(car => car.origin, opt=>opt.MapFrom(carDto =>
carDto.Origin))
.ReverseMap();
```

Notice that for every member that we want to share between the DTO and the POCO class, there is an entry. At the bottom is ReverseMap, which, as you may have guessed, reverses the mapping (for example, it causes the map to go from **DTO > Car** to **Car > DTO**).

We have taken care of the DTO; now we need to connect our POCO to the database. We'll do that with Dapper.

Dapper

As noted earlier, we will use Dapper as our **Object Relational Model** (**ORM**). This will greatly simplify our interaction between the repository and the database. Dapper has its own syntax but it is very (very) close to SQL and the points of departure will be obvious.

> **Installing Dapper**
>
> To install and use Dapper, please see their very straightforward and comprehensive instructions at https://www.learndapper.com/

Here, for example, is the Dapper code to get a car by ID:

```
Public async Task<Car?> GetCarById(int carId)
{
var sql =
    $@"SELECT *
        FROM
            Cars C
        WHERE
            C.id = @{nameof(carId)}
            AND C.is_deleted = 0";

var param = new
  {
```

```
    carId
};

var car = await QueryFirstOrDefaultAsync<Car>(sql, param);

return car;
}
```

We can create more complex statements with conditional logic.

> **Note**
> Dapper uses C# rather than SQL syntax except for the query itself. This makes interacting with the database much easier for C# programmers.

That is really all you need to know to get started creating your API. Let's try inserting a car into the database using the API.

Examining the SQL

The SQL (pronounced See-Quill) in the above example can almost be read as an English sentence. First, we use the keyword SELECT to indicate that we want to pick out and return a subset of the data in the Database.

Next comes the asterisk (*) which indicates that we want all the columns. The alternative is to list the columns we want.

`From Cars C` indicates that we want the data to come from the `Cars` table, and that we will be using the alias C to refer to that table.

The `Where` statement constrains the search to the criteria that follows it, in this case where the id of the car (using the alias C) matches the id we're looking for. We then tack on "`where is_deleted = 0`" indicating that we only want entries that are not marked as deleted.

Here is where Dapper comes in. We set up an array of parameters, and then

call: `QueryFirstOrDefaultAsync<Car>(sql, param);`

This invokes the `QueryFirstOrDefault` method in dapper. We pass in the type of object we are looking for (Car) and then two parameters. For our purposes, the first will always be SQL, and the second will always be the name of the collection we created above (param).

We assign the result (in this case one car) to a variable, and return that value.

Please note that the constructor for this class will have interfaces passed in through Dependency Injection, and those parameters will be assigned to member variables (for example, _carService). If you are not familiar with Dependency Injection, please refer to the code in the repository.

Putting it all together (inserting a car)

Let's put this together using controller, service, and repository to insert a car with Dapper and AutoMapper:

```
//Controller
[HttpPost]
 public async Task<ActionResult<Car>> Insert([FromBody] CarDto
 carAsDto)
 {
     try
     {
         if (carAsDto == null)
         {
             return BadRequest("No car was provided");
         }

         var carToInsert = _mapper.Map<Car>(carAsDto);
         var insertedCar = await _carService.Insert(carToInsert);
         var insertedCarDto = _mapper.Map<CarDto>(insertedCar);
         var location = $"https://localhost:5001/car/{insertedCarDto.
         Id}";
         return Created(location, insertedCarDto);
     }
     catch (Exception e)
     {
         return StatusCode(StatusCodes.Status500InternalServerError);
     }
 }
```

Notice that we've transformed the DTO to a database object (Car), which we then pass to the service:

```
// car service
 public async Task<Car> Insert(Car)
 {
     var newId = await _carRepository.UpsertAsync(car);
     if (newId > 0)
     {
         car.id = newId;
     }
     else
     {
         throw new Exception("Failed to insert car");
     }
     return car;
 }
```

We are now ready to pass this car to the repository for storage in our database:

```
public async Task<int> UpsertAsync(Car car)
  {
      using var db = databaseConnectionFactory.GetConnection();
      var sql = @"
      DECLARE @InsertedRows AS TABLE (Id int);
      MERGE INTO Car AS target
      USING (SELECT @Id AS Id, @Name AS Name, @MPG as MPG, @
      Cylinders as Cylinders, @Displacement as Displacement, @
      Horsepower as Horsepower, @Weight as Weight, @Acceleration as
      Acceleration, @Model_Year AS Model_Year, @Origin AS origin, @
      Is_Deleted AS Is_Deleted ) AS source
      ON target.Id = source.Id
      WHEN MATCHED THEN
          UPDATE SET
              Name = source.Name,
              MPG = source.MPG,
              Cylinders = source.Cylinders,
              Displacement = source.Displacement,
              Horsepower = source.Horsepower,
              Weight = source.Weight,
              Acceleration = source.Acceleration,
              Model_Year = source.Model_Year,
              Origin = source.Origin,
              Is_Deleted = source.Is_Deleted
      WHEN NOT MATCHED THEN
          INSERT (Name, Mpg, Cylinders, Displacement, Horsepower,
          Weight, Acceleration, Model_Year, Origin, Is_deleted)
          VALUES (source.Name, source.MPG, source.Cylinders, source.
          Displacement, source.Horsepower, source.Weight, source.
          Acceleration, source.Model_Year, source.Origin, source.Is_
          Deleted)
          OUTPUT inserted.Id INTO @InsertedRows
      ;

      SELECT Id FROM @InsertedRows;
  ";

      var newId = await db.QuerySingleOrDefaultAsync<int>(sql, car);
      return newId == 0 ? car.id : newId;
  }
```

If we get a valid new car, we pass back the newId value, which we check for in the service. However, that is a lot of data we are passing to the API. We'll look at solving that problem in the next section.

A note on dependency injection: as you know, we pass in interfaces to our methods so that we can support dependency injection. This is set up in Program.cs, and the injection itself is automatic.

Creating the body in Postman

As you can see, the data that we want to pass into the API will be too much for the query string, and so we will pass it into the body. We can signal this in the definition of the API by writing the following:

```
public async Task<ActionResult<Car>> Insert([FromBody] CarDto
carAsDto)
```

Every API call will have zero or more FromQuery, FromUrl, and FromBody attributes. In this case, we are just using FromBody. Our call through Postman is seen in *Figure 3.4*:

Figure 3.4 – Inserting a car

Here, we are inserting all the properties of the car (except the ID value) as seen in the top window. To do this, we would adjust the SQL statement to take all the properties. Notice that the API returns the properties of the inserted car, including its id (bottom window). The return code will be 201 (created).

Since we are looking for the data in the body of the request, the URL is just the address of the controller.

We have inserted a single car, but I have pre-seeded the database with many more. Let's use the API to see them.

Get all

To get a list of all the cars in the database, we begin in the controller:

Warning: the following example shows calling the repository directly for illustration purposes. Shortly afterwards we will discuss the correct way to do this.

```
public async Task<IEnumerable<Car>> GetAll(bool returnDeletedRecords =
false)
{
    return await _carRepository.GetAll(returnDeletedRecords);
}
```

Here, we call the repository directly. This is an alternative to calling the service, and is generally a bad practice, but I wanted to show how it is done. Notice that we include a Boolean parameter as to whether to return the deleted records as well.

Normally, we would use a Service class for separation of concerns. The service class would contain the program logic and would sit between the controller and the repository.

In the repository, we build our SqlBuilder (as we saw earlier in the section on *Dapper*) and obtain the records:

```
public async Task<IEnumerable<Car>> GetAll(bool returnDeletedRecords =
false)
{
    var builder = new SqlBuilder();
    var sqlTemplate = builder.AddTemplate("SELECT * FROM car " +
    "/**where**/ ");
    if (!returnDeletedRecords)
    {
        builder.Where("is_deleted=0");
    }
    using var db = databaseConnectionFactory.GetConnection();
    return await db.QueryAsync<Car>(sqlTemplate.RawSql,sqlTemplate.
    Parameters)
}
```

Let's take that one line at a time. The first line indicates that we will return a list of Car objects and the decision as to whether or not to return deleted records defaults to false.

We next create a SqlBuilder object and then set the SqlTemplate object to select everything from the car.

Notice the /**where**/ statement. This is a Dapper convention indicating that a where clause may be placed here.

We will now check to see whether the deleted records are to be included, and if not, we add a where clause using the builder we created on the first line.

We are ready to get the Database from the factory we created and then query the database, passing in the RawSql code created for use in the SqlTemplate object and the parameters. In this case, there are no parameters.

What we get back is an array of Car objects, which we return to the calling method.

To test this, we set Postman to Get and the URL to https://localhost:7025/Car. Since no ID is provided, our code will get them all, as shown in *Figure 3.5*:

```
Pretty    Raw    Preview    Visualize    JSON  ˅

1    [
2        {
3            "id": 1,
4            "name": "chevrolet chevelle malibu",
5            "mpg": "18",
6            "cylinders": "8",
7            "displacement": "307",
8            "horsepower": "130",
9            "weight": "3504",
10           "acceleration": "12",
11           "model_year": "70",
12           "origin": "usa",
13           "is_deleted": "0"
14       },
15       {
16           "id": 2,
17           "name": "buick skylark 320",
18           "mpg": "15",
19           "cylinders": "8",
20           "displacement": "350",
21           "horsepower": "165",
22           "weight": "3693",
23           "acceleration": "11.5",
24           "model_year": "70",
```

Figure 3.5 – Getting all the cars in the database

Having inserted records, we may want to change one or another. To do that, we'll want to use the Put verb.

Update

Updating uses the HTTP Put verb. Let's trace through how it is done.

We return to the controller and add an HttpPut attribute. We then indicate that the contents will be in the body of the request (rather than the query) as we saw in the insert:

```
[HttpPut]
public async Task<IActionResult> Put([FromBody] Car car)
```

Since we can't be certain that the record we want to update is still in the database, we put the call in a try block, and if we get an exception, we call BadRequest. Interestingly, if we succeed, we call NoContent as we are not adding anything to the database:

```
[HttpPut]
public async Task<IActionResult> Put([FromBody] Car car)
{
    try
    {
        await _carService.Update(car);
    }
    catch (Exception e)
    {
        return BadRequest(e);
    }

    return NoContent();
}
```

As shown, from here we call the carService's Update method, passing in the car we want to update. Note that some programmers use OK rather than NoContent.

In the service, we'll make sure we got a valid car id value and then call UpsertAsync, passing in the car. If we get back any id value except the original, we throw an exception; otherwise, we return the Car object:

```
public async Task<Car> Update(Car car)
{
    if (car.id == 0)
    {
        throw new Exception("Id must be set");
    }
```

```
    var oldId = car.id;

    var newId = await _carRepository.UpsertAsync(car);

    if (newId != oldId)
    {
        throw new Exception("Failed to update car");
    }
    return car;
}
```

In the `Upsert` method, we check to see whether this is a new car (insert) or an update:

```
public async Task<int> UpsertAsync(Car car)
{
    using var db = databaseConnectionFactory.GetConnection();
    var sql = @"
DECLARE @InsertedRows AS TABLE (Id int);
MERGE INTO Car AS target
USING (SELECT @Id AS Id, @Name AS Name, @MPG as MPG, @Cylinders as
Cylinders, @Displacement as Displacement, @Horsepower as
Horsepower, @Weight as Weight, @Acceleration as Acceleration, @
Model_Year AS Model_Year, @Origin AS origin, @Is_Deleted AS Is_
Deleted ) AS source
ON target.Id = source.Id
WHEN MATCHED THEN
    UPDATE SET
        Name = source.Name,
        MPG = source.MPG,
        Cylinders = source.Cylinders,
        Displacement = source.Displacement,
        Horsepower = source.Horsepower,
        Weight = source.Weight,
        Acceleration = source.Acceleration,
        Model_Year = source.Model_Year,
        Origin = source.Origin,
        Is_Deleted = source.Is_Deleted
WHEN NOT MATCHED THEN
    INSERT (Name, Mpg, Cylinders, Displacement, Horsepower,
    Weight, Acceleration, Model_Year, Origin, Is_deleted)
    VALUES (source.Name, source.MPG, source.Cylinders, source.
    Displacement, source.Horsepower, source.Weight, source.
    Acceleration, source.Model_Year, source.Origin, source.Is_
```

```
            Deleted)
            OUTPUT inserted.Id INTO @InsertedRows
        ;

        SELECT Id FROM @InsertedRows;
    ";

        var newId = await db.QuerySingleOrDefaultAsync<int>(sql, car);
        return newId == 0 ? car.id : newId;
    }
```

Notice, in the final two lines, that we obtain the `newId` value from the query and if it is 0, we return the original car ID. Otherwise, we return the `newid` value from the car we inserted.

Soft delete

For the sake of completeness, let's take a quick look at soft delete. You'll remember that when the user asks to delete a record, rather than actually removing it from the database, we mark it as deleted (in the `is_deleted` column) so that we can obtain those records as needed.

We start back in the controller:

```
[HttpDelete("{id}")]
public async Task<IActionResult> Delete(int id)
{
    try
    {
        await _carService.Delete(id);
    }
    catch (Exception e)
    {
        return BadRequest(e);
    }
    return NoContent();
}
```

`Delete` takes the ID of the car to mark as deleted and then calls the service. All the service does is make sure that the ID is valid and then call the repository to do the actual deletion:

```
public async Task Delete(int id)
{
    var car = await _carRepository.Get(id);

    if (car == null)
```

```
    {
        throw new Exception("Car not found");
    }

    await _carRepository.DeleteAsync(id);

    return;
}
```

The code in the repo is dead simple. It gets the connection to the database and creates the query to set is_deleted to 1. It then executes that query:

```
public async Task<int> DeleteAsync(int id)
{
    using var db = databaseConnectionFactory.GetConnection();
    var query = "UPDATE car SET Is_Deleted = 1 WHERE Id = @Id";
    return await db.ExecuteAsync(query, new { Id = id });
}
```

At this point, you have a complete API for **Create, Read, Update, Delete (CRUD)** operations.

Summary

In this chapter, you were introduced to using Dapper and AutoMapper, the latter for DTO objects. You also dove into the workings of the CRUD operations, using the typical three classes: controller, service, and repository.

You saw that for simple operations, you can bypass the Service, but this is considered bad practice.

In an enterprise application, you will want to use DTOs to separate the layout of the database from the layout of the object being passed around. As we delve into the realm of enhancing API usability and understanding, the next chapter will highlight the significance of documenting your project with Swagger.

You try it

Create a simple database to track your music collection. Put this in a database and use Dapper and AutoMapper to implement the four CRUD operations. For this exercise, create DTOs that provide only a subset of the columns in the database.

Minimal APIs

Minimal APIs offer an alternative way to create APIs without using Controllers. While they still allow for the injection of required services, they are primarily intended for smaller endpoints with minimal dependencies.

In contrast, Controllers come with a larger hierarchy of endpoint components to consider. This includes features such as versioning, controller naming, and manual route attributes, which can introduce extra boilerplate that may not always be necessary. Minimal APIs simplify this process by allowing you to declare and handle requests in a single expression.

To illustrate, let's reimplement the call to get all cars. Start with the code from *Chapter 3*, then use the app variable to add calls to `MapGet`. The route will be `/car-minimal`, and the handler can remain the same as the `GetAll` method: a call to `ICarRepository.GetAll`. But how will we access the service interface without a constructor? Minimal APIs solve this by using parameter injection. Simply pass `ICarRepository carRepository` as an argument to the delegate for `MapGet` parameter, and use it to call the `.GetAll` method.

Many different types can be injected into the handlers for Minimal APIs. Model-bound types are differentiated by applying attributes to individual parameters. Commonly used ones include `[FromRoute]`, `[FromBody]`, and `[FromServices]`. Additional special types include `HttpContext`, `HttpRequest`, `HttpResponse`, `IFormFile`, and a `Stream` of the request body. The full list is available in the official Microsoft documentation.

4

Documentation with Swagger

In this chapter, we'll look at documenting your project with Swagger. Human-readable documentation is critical in an API. It allows your clients to understand each endpoint and the potential responses quickly.

We'll ensure that our Swagger documentation adheres to the OpenAPI (formerly Swagger) Specification by utilizing XML and incorporating attributes within the code. You can learn more about OpenAPI at `https://swagger.io/docs/specification/about/`.

Swagger needs an OpenAPI implementation, and in the case of .NET, Swashbuckle serves as the designated option.

In this chapter, we will cover the following topics:

- What Swagger is
- How Swagger is used
- How to set up Swagger
- How to pass parameters to Swagger

Technical requirements

For this chapter, all you will need is Visual Studio. All of the features we'll be using come with Visual Studio, or can be obtained for free through NuGet.

The code files for this book are available in the book's GitHub repository : `https://github.com/PacktPublishing/Programming-APIs-with-C-Sharp-and-.NET/tree/main/Chapter04`

Setting up the Swagger documentation

To install Swagger, open your solution and from the menu, select **Tools** | **NuGet Package Manager** | **Manage NuGet Packages for Solution**. Install the latest version of `Swashbuckle.AspNetCore`.

Right-click on your project file and click on **Properties**. On the left of your screen, choose **Application**. On the right, choose **Console Application**, as shown in *Figure 4.1*:

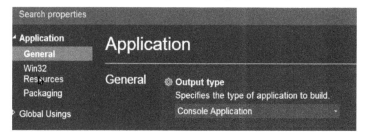

Figure 4.1 – Installation part 1

Under **Build**, choose **Output** and scroll down to **Documentation file**. Check the **Generate a file containing API documentation** box, as shown in *Figure 4.2*:

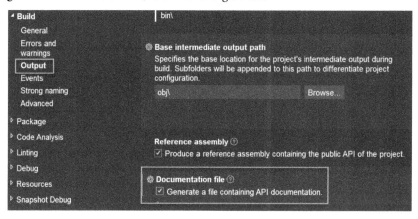

Figure 4.2 – Setting up Swagger output

> **Note**
>
> In *Figure 4.2*, **Generate a file containing API documentation** is checked. The file that is generated can be imported into other applications, such as Postman, for an integrated documentation and testing experience.

Open `Program.cs` (typically the last file in Solution Explorer) and add the Swagger generator to the services collection:

```
builder.Services.AddSwaggerGen(
  x =>
  {
      x.SwaggerDoc(
```

```
        "v1",
    new OpenApiInfo
    {
        Title = $"{Assembly.GetExecutingAssembly().GetName().
        Name}",
        Version = "Version 1",
        Description = "Create documentation for Cars",
        Contact = new OpenApiContact
        {
            Name = "Jesse Liberty",
            Email = "jesseliberty@gmail.com",
            Url = new Uri("https://jesseliberty.com")
        }
    });
        var xmlFilename = System.IO.Path.Combine(System.
        AppContext.BaseDirectory, $"{Assembly.
        GetExecutingAssembly().GetName().Name}.xml");
        x.IncludeXmlComments(xmlFilename);

});
```

Save everything. That's it. This is only done once. You have now set up Swagger documentation. In fact, you've already added the description, name, and contact information. The result is shown in *Figure 4.3*. This is what you will see when you start your program and Swagger opens a browser window to display its interface:

Figure 4.3 – Top of Swagger documentation

Notice that on this page, the website and email are live links and the text Create documentation for Cars is what you put in the description in the preceding code.

Swagger for the controller

Swagger documentation is implemented using XML comments. XML comments are preceded by three slash marks. Here's an example:

```
/// XML comment
```

XML comments are paired tags, such as the following:

```
/// <summary>
...
/// </summary>
```

Let's start with the controller of our Cars application. We're going to put Swagger documentation above every method in the controller.

The first comment we'll add is the summary:

```
/// <summary>
/// Get all the cars in the Database
/// </summary>
```

This comment will appear next to the route for the **GET** button, as shown in *Figure 4.4*:

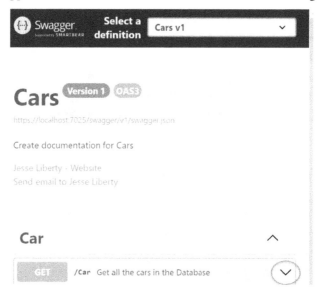

Figure 4.4 – Display the summary

Before we go any further, let's look at what we get from Swagger without writing any additional code.

Swagger out of the box

Note that Swagger will come up automatically just after you start your application.

To see the auto-generated documentation, click on the arrow on the far right as circled in *Figure 4.4*. Swagger opens the details of the **Get** command, as shown in *Figure 4.5*:

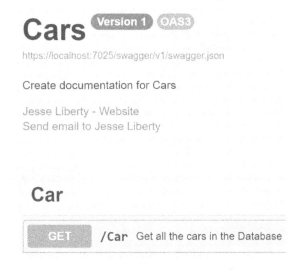

Figure 4.5 – Swagger out of the box

This is a little hard to see, so let's zoom in on a couple of important parts. In the upper-left corner is an area for all the parameters you'll be sending in for the `GetAll` command. We are sending in `returnDeletedRecords` with a default value of `false`. *Figure 4.6* shows how Swagger depicts this:

Figure 4.6 – Parameters

Notice the dropdown. It lets you try out both possible values (`false` and `true`).

Next, on the left side are the code and description for the potential responses from the server. *Figure 4.7* shows that the first potential response is `200: Success`:

Responses

Code	Description
200	Success

Figure 4.7 – Success

Beneath the first response code is the schema that tells you what properties there are and what their type is, as shown in *Figure 4.8*:

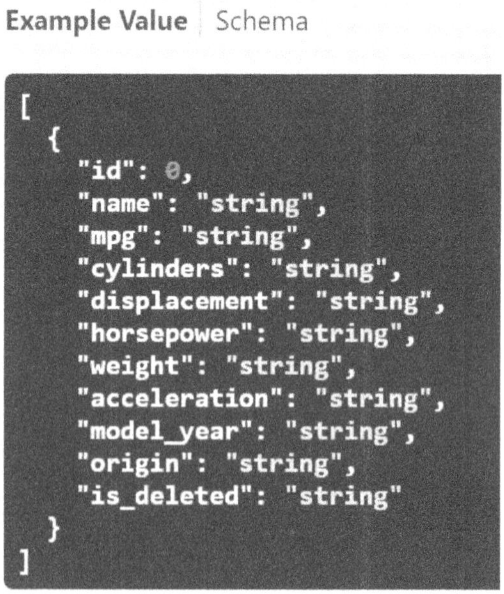

Example Value | Schema

```
[
    {
        "id": 0,
        "name": "string",
        "mpg": "string",
        "cylinders": "string",
        "displacement": "string",
        "horsepower": "string",
        "weight": "string",
        "acceleration": "string",
        "model_year": "string",
        "origin": "string",
        "is_deleted": "string"
    }
]
```

Figure 4.8 – Schema

We are all set to see the effects of our comments. Let's take a look at what happens when we start the application and Swagger comes up.

Running your API in Swagger

Most importantly, in the upper-right corner is a **Try It Out** button. Clicking on this button puts Swagger into interactive mode, and allows you to try out your code. When that button is clicked, two other buttons appear: **Execute** and **Clear**. Pressing **Execute** causes the code to run and in our case returns the list of cars, along with some other metadata. Let's zero in on that (**Clear** removes the results so that you can try again).

The first thing we see is marked as **Curl**, as shown in *Figure 4.9*:

Curl

```
curl -X 'GET' \
  'https://localhost:7025/Car?returnDeletedRecords=false' \
  -H 'accept: text/plain'
```

Figure 4.9 – Every Swagger page displays the curl for the endpoint

According to Wikipedia, "*Curl combines text markup (as in HTML), scripting (as in JavaScript), and heavy-duty computing (as in Java, C#, or C++) within one unified framework*". We will be ignoring Curl in this book.

Below that, we see the request URL that we submitted to the server, as shown in *Figure 4.10*:

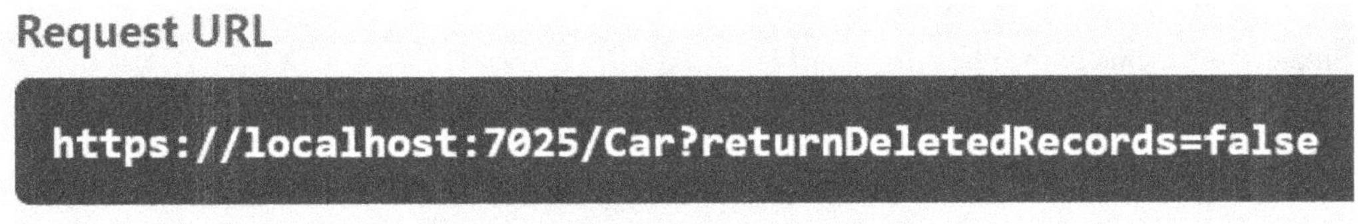

Request URL

```
https://localhost:7025/Car?returnDeletedRecords=false
```

Figure 4.10 – Request URL as displayed in Swagger

Notice that we are working with port 7025 (yours may differ) on localhost and that we pass our parameter (`returnDeletedRecords=false`) as we would with any HTML.

Next comes the most important server response: the response body, as shown in *Figure 4.11*:

Figure 4.11 – Server response

Finally, the schema of the response object is displayed, as shown in *Figure 4.12*:

Example Value | Schema

```
[
    {
        "id": 0,
        "name": "string",
        "mpg": "string",
        "cylinders": "string",
        "displacement": "string",
        "horsepower": "string",
        "weight": "string",
        "acceleration": "string",
        "model_year": "string",
        "origin": "string",
        "is_deleted": "string"
    }
]
```

Figure 4.12 – Response schema

Swagger is terrific for documentation, but somewhat limited as a way to test your application. As we'll see, Postman is a much more powerful application for testing.

param tag

If your verb has parameters, you can document them in the Swagger attributes using the `param` keyword. For example, in our case, we want to document the `returnDeletedRecords` parameter. We can do so like this:

```
/// <summary>
/// Get all the cars in the Database
/// </summary>
/// <param name="returnDeletedRecords">If true, the method will return
all the records, including the ones that have been deleted</param>
```

The result is that the parameter is documented in Swagger, as shown in *Figure 4.13*:

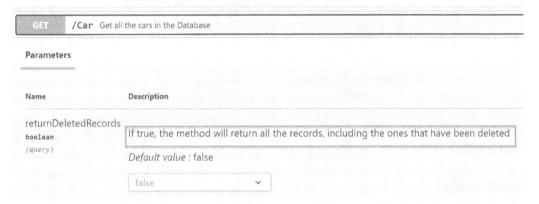

Figure 4.13 – Documenting the parameters

Response codes

You can (and should) document all the possible response codes and what they indicate:

```
/// <response code="200">Cars returned</response>
/// <response code="404">Specified Car not found</response>
/// <response code="500">An Internal Server Error prevented the
request from being executed.</response>
```

The result is that the return codes are documented in Swagger, as shown in *Figure 4.14*:

Figure 4.14 – Documenting the return codes

While this all takes a bit of effort, it becomes routine and is a best practice. It also makes the lives of your clients far easier.

Summary

In this chapter, you learned how to set up Swashbuckle to enable Swagger. Swagger provides extensive documentation of your API, allowing (human) clients to learn about each endpoint and what it is for. In addition, you can also document each parameter and the potential error codes.

In the next chapter, you'll see how we can validate endpoint requests on the way in – preventing wasted resources and protecting you from various attacks against your system.

You try it

Install Swagger and create the documentation for the `Insert` endpoint in the `Car` controller. Run Swagger to ensure that all your documentation is displayed properly.

5

Data Validation

Sending data from your API to the database only to find out that the input is invalid is unnecessarily expensive. Far better is to test the data on the way in to make sure it meets basic criteria. This preliminary set of tests (known as validation) examines the input data to make sure it meets the minimum criteria and that it is formatted properly.

In this chapter, you will learn the following:

- How to validate input data
- How to respond to invalid data

Technical requirements

For this chapter, create a new branch off the existing **data transfer object** (DTO) branch (so that we start with valid data). You will need the following:

- **Visual Studio**
- AutoMapper
- FluentValidation

The FluentValidation library is a powerful tool for creating validators that we will use throughout this chapter. You can install it in various ways, but the easiest is as a NuGet package. You'll also want the package for ASP.NET, as shown in *Figure 5.1*:

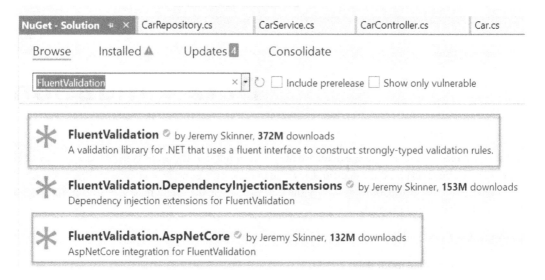

Figure 5.1 – NuGet installation

You can find the complete documentation for FluentValidation at https://docs.fluentvalidation.net/en/latest/index.html#. I will provide detailed steps as we go along.

The code files for this chapter can be found in the GitHub repository here: https://github.com/PacktPublishing/Programming-APIs-with-C-Sharp-and-.NET/tree/main/Chapter05

Tuning your API

Now that we have the fundamentals for our program, we want to validate the data that is coming in, both to speed things up and to protect against malicious data. We can do that with validation, but first, we need to make a couple of changes to give us good code to work with.

Paging

Remember that we are simulating an automobile buying and selling application. There can be literally hundreds of cars in our database. We need to add paging to our Get endpoint so that when we get the list of vehicles, they don't all come down at once. This will also give us something to validate.

To facilitate this, we need to know the following:

- How big the page is – that is, the number of cars on each page
- The index of the page the client wants to see

We'll accomplish this by modifying our Get endpoint to take two additional parameters:

- pageOffset
- pageSize

Both of these are int data types, as shown here:

```
[HttpGet]
public async Task<IEnumerable<Car>> Get([FromRoute] bool showDeleted,
int pageNumber, int pageSize )
```

The first new parameter (pageNumber) will tell Get which page it is on, and the second (pageSize) will tell how many rows to get. Let's look at an example in Postman, as shown in *Figure 5.2*:

| GET | ∨ | https://localhost:7025/Car?returnDeletedRecords=false&pageNumber=0&pageSize=3 |

Figure 5.2 – Paging

Here, we have set pageNumber to 0, indicating we want to start at the beginning of the list, and pageSize to 3, indicating we want only three records. As a result, the API will extract the first three records. If we set pageNumber to 3, we will get records 10, 11, and 12 (that is, start at the fourth page and get the next three records).

One enhancement you might want to make to reduce confusion for the user is to subtract 1 from the page number to get the offset. This will allow the user to enter Page 1 for offset 0.

Validation

It is a best practice to validate the incoming properties on your endpoint *before* executing the associated method. This not only increases the performance of the API, but it also protects you from some forms of hacking (for example, injection).

Our recommendation is to use the FluentValidation NuGet package, which you can install as shown in the *Technical requirements* section at the start of this chapter.

Once installed, you have many options as to how to capture errors. Let's look at a few.

Capturing errors

You'll remember that our `Car` object (defined in *Chapter 3*) looks like this:

```
public class Car
{
    public int id { get; set; }
    public string name { get; set; }
    public string mpg { get; set; }
    public string cylinders { get; set; }
    public string displacement { get; set; }
    public string horsepower { get; set; }
    public string weight { get; set; }
    public string acceleration { get; set; }
    public string model_year { get; set; }
    public string origin { get; set; }
    public string? is_deleted { get; set;}
}
```

Let's also say that cars must not be deleted. You can create a validator for that pretty quickly. First, add a `Using` statement:

```
Using FluentValidation
```

Next, create a class that derives from `AbstractValidator`:

```
public class CarDtoValidator : AbstractValidator<Car>
```

Finally, put your validation rules in the constructor for that class. Each rule is created by using the `RuleFor` keyword and a lambda expression that indicates which property you want to validate and the validation rule. Our simple example will look like this:

```
using Cars.Data.DTOs;
using FluentValidation;

namespace Cars.Validators
{
    public class CarDtoValidator : AbstractValidator<CarDto>
    {
        public CarDtoValidator()
        {
            RuleFor(x => x.Is_Deleted).Equal("0");
        }
    }
}
```

The Equal operator is one of many that you can find on the FluentValidation documentation page: https://docs.fluentvalidation.net/en/latest/built-in-validators.html.

We'll test the data and then either compare it to what is valid and return an error if appropriate, or, more commonly, we'll throw an exception if the data fails validation.

Testing the return value

There are a number of ways to deal with a validation error. One is to return an error to the calling method. Thus, to validate a Car object, conceptually you want the following:

```
CarDto car = new CarDto();
CarDtoValidator carDtoValidator = new CarDtoValidator ();
carDtoValidator.Validate(car);
```

In our insert method, we'll check to make sure CarDto is valid (in this case, that it is not deleted):

```
[HttpPost]
public async Task<ActionResult<Car>> Insert([FromBody] CarDto
carAsDto)
{
    try
    {
        if (carAsDto == null)
        {
            return BadRequest("No car was provided");
        }

        CarDtoValidator validator = new CarDtoValidator();
        var result = validator.Validate(carAsDto);
        if (!result.IsValid)
        {
            return BadRequest(result.Errors);
        }

        var carToInsert = _mapper.Map<Car>(carAsDto);
        var insertedCar = await _carService.Insert(carToInsert);
        var insertedCarDto = _mapper.Map<CarDto>(insertedCar);
        var location = $"https://localhost:5001/car/
        {insertedCarDto.Id}";
        return Created(location, insertedCarDto);
    }
    catch (Exception e)
    {
```

```
        return StatusCode(StatusCodes.Status500InternalServerError);
    }
}
```

Let's take a look at returning an error code for data that fails our validation check.

Returning an error

If we now send CarDto to the endpoint using Postman but set Is_Deleted to 1, we will get an error as shown in *Figure 5.3*:

```
Body    Cookies    Headers (4)    Test Results                          Status: 400 Bad Request

Pretty    Raw    Preview    Visualize    JSON  ∨    ⇥

1   [
2   │    {
3   │        "propertyName": "Is_Deleted",
4   │        "errorMessage": "'Is_ Deleted' must be equal to '0'.",
5   │        "attemptedValue": "1",
6   │        "customState": null,
7   │        "severity": 0,
8   │        "errorCode": "EqualValidator",
9   │        "formattedMessagePlaceholderValues": {
10  │            "ComparisonValue": "0",
11  │            "ComparisonProperty": "",
12  │            "PropertyName": "Is_ Deleted",
13  │            "PropertyValue": "1",
14  │            "PropertyPath": "Is_Deleted"
15  │        }
16  │    }
17  ]
```

Figure 5.3 – Validation error

Notice that the return HTTP value is 400 – Bad Request. This makes sense as the DTO passed in was not valid.

Adding a custom message

This input is great and provides a lot of information, but the 1 value that is in the Is_Deleted field has meaning; specifically that the record is already deleted. This fails the validation check.

We can make the error clearer with a custom message. Return to CarDtoValidator and modify the rule as follows:

```
RuleFor(x => x.Is_Deleted).Equal("0").WithMessage("Car must not be
deleted");
```

You can see a new error message in *Figure 5.4*:

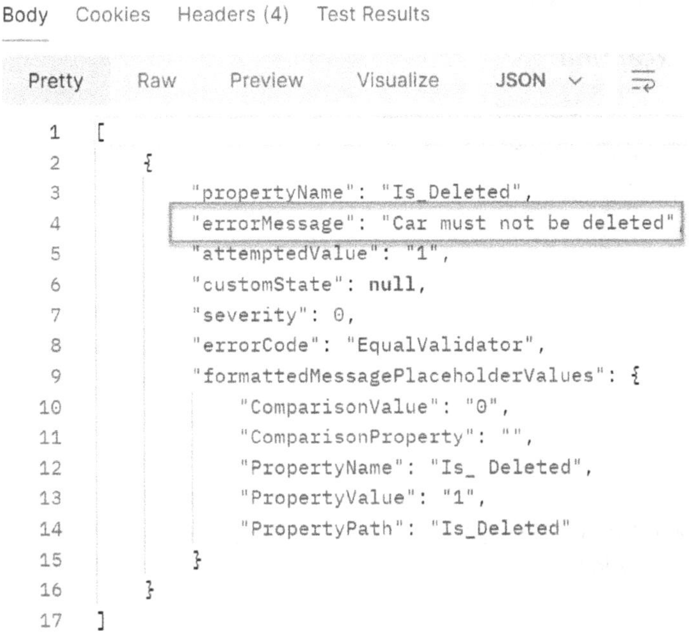

```json
1  [
2      {
3          "propertyName": "Is_Deleted",
4          "errorMessage": "Car must not be deleted",
5          "attemptedValue": "1",
6          "customState": null,
7          "severity": 0,
8          "errorCode": "EqualValidator",
9          "formattedMessagePlaceholderValues": {
10             "ComparisonValue": "0",
11             "ComparisonProperty": "",
12             "PropertyName": "Is_ Deleted",
13             "PropertyValue": "1",
14             "PropertyPath": "Is_Deleted"
15         }
16     }
17 ]
```

Figure 5.4 – Custom error message

Custom messages provide vital information to your client. They help avoid confusion and make immediately clear what is wrong with the submitted data.

Chaining

If you want to validate more than one aspect of a property, you can chain tests using the dot operator:

```
RuleFor(x=> x.Is_Deleted).NotEmpty().Equal("0").WithMessage("Car must
not be deleted");
```

This test ensures that the `Is_Deleted` field is not empty and also verifies that its value is equal to 0, and returns an error message if the submitted value is not valid.

The default is that even if the first test (`NotEmpty`) fails, the second test will run (`Equal("0")`). You can prevent this by using `CascadeMode`.

If you do not want the second test (`NotEmpty`) to run if the first test (`Is_Deleted`) fails, use `CascadeMode.Stop` as shown here:

```
RuleFor(x=> x.Is_Deleted).Cascade(CascadeMode.Stop).NotEmpty().
Equal("0").WithMessage("Car must not be deleted");
```

This now works like && in C# – that is, if the first test fails the second is never evaluated. The two values for `CascadeMode` are `Stop` and `Continue`, with the latter being the default.

Throwing an exception

As an alternative to validating and then checking the result, you can call `ValidateAndThrow`. With this terser expression each of your rules will be evaluated, and if one fails, an exception will be thrown:

```
CarDtoValidator validator = new CarDtoValidator();
//var result = validator.Validate(carAsDto);

//if (!result.IsValid)
//{
//    return BadRequest(result.Errors);
//}

validator.ValidateAndThrow(carAsDto);
```

The exception that is thrown is of type `ValidationException`, so you can test for that in your `catch` blocks. In addition, that exception has an `Errors` property, which has the error message for your failed attempt.

In the next code snippet, you can see how to set up to throw an exception if the validation fails. We create the validator and then call `ValidateAndThrow`, passing in the `Dto` object. You can then catch that exception and examine the errors:

```
try
{
    if (carAsDto == null)
    {
        return BadRequest("No car was provided");
    }

    CarDtoValidator validator = new CarDtoValidator();

    validator.ValidateAndThrow(carAsDto);

    //...
}
catch(ValidationException e)
{
    IEnumerable<ValidationFailure> errors = e.Errors;
    return BadRequest(errors);
}
catch (Exception e)
```

```
{
    return StatusCode(StatusCodes.Status500InternalServerError);
}
```

To save you the time and effort of creating custom validators for common scenarios, FluentValidation provides a number of built-in validators.

Built-in validators

There is a cornucopia of built-in validators in addition to the Equal and NotEmpty validators we've seen so far. I won't provide a comprehensive list (see the documentation) but one of the most interesting is the PredicateValidator validator. This passes the value of the property to a delegate, which can use custom validation logic. This is accomplished with the keyword Must keyword, as shown here:

```
RuleFor(car => car.Is_Deleted).Must(isDeleted => isDeleted == "0").
WithMessage("Car must have value zero");
```

If this validation fails, the issue is displayed in the results as shown in *Figure 5.5*:

Body   Cookies   Headers (4)   Test Results   Status: 400 Bad Request

Pretty   Raw   Preview   Visualize   JSON ∨   ⇄

```
1   [
2       {
3           "propertyName": "Is_Deleted",
4           "errorMessage": "Car must have value zero",
5           "attemptedValue": "1",
6           "customState": null,
7           "severity": 0,
8           "errorCode": "PredicateValidator",
9           "formattedMessagePlaceholderValues": {
10              "PropertyName": "Is_ Deleted",
11              "PropertyValue": "1",
12              "PropertyPath": "Is_Deleted"
13          }
14      }
15  ]
```

Figure 5.5 – PredicateValidator error

There is a `RegularExpression` validator that uses the `Matches` keyword (instead of `Must`), but one of my favorites is `EmailValidator`, which ensures that the value submitted is a valid email. Similarly, there is a `CreditCard` validator:

```
RuleFor(cc => cc.CreditCard).CreditCard();
```

There are quite a few more, such as `NotNull`, `NotEmpty`, `Equal`, `NotEqual`, and so forth.

The best place to see a complete list of built-in validators and how to use them is in the `FluentValidation` documentation: `https://docs.fluentvalidation.net/en/latest/index.html#`.

Summary

In this chapter, you saw how to use `FluentValidation` to validate input properties before executing code for the API.

You saw how to create rules, how to chain them, and how to ensure that a second rule in a chain is not evaluated if the first fails.

You learned two ways of dealing with errors – testing the return error or throwing an exception – and you saw how to create a custom error message.

In the next chapter, we will turn our attention to Azure Functions – a critical part of programming APIs in .NET. Following that, we will look at Durable Azure Functions and what they add to Azure Functions.

You try it

Create a set of rules for the `Car` class (or another class you create) and throw an exception if a validation rule is violated. Ensure that the failure of the validation is handled.

As a bonus, create a predicate (`must`) custom rule and test against that.

6

Azure Functions

Determining the execution environment of your APIs can have a large impact on how they run, how they scale, how much they cost, and what features come out of the box. Azure Functions provides a different hosting option that complements existing Azure services with a focus on event-driven execution. While Functions provides many ways to react to different things in a system, we'll focus on a specific event: the HTTP request.

In this chapter, we'll cover some technical aspects related to hosting and billing and finish with a walkthrough that includes cloud deployment and configuration.

By the end of this chapter, you'll have a good base to continue your API journey by knowing about the following aspects:

- Hosting considerations that affect certain runtime options and limitations based on the needs of your application.
- How certain aspects of your application can affect billing.
- The structure, general familiarity, and possibilities of code design related specifically to HTTP APIs.
- Deploying to Azure from Visual Studio. Automated builds, continuous integration, and continuous delivery will be covered later in this book.
- Making runtime configuration changes without redeployment.
- How to adjust scaling settings to reduce the potential cost of a public endpoint, colloquially known as a Denial-of-Wallet attack.

Technical requirements

To build Azure Functions in Visual Studio, you'll need the Azure development workload available in Visual Studio Installer. The source code for this chapter is available at `https://github.com/PacktPublishing/Programming-APIs-with-C-Sharp-and-.NET/tree/main/Chapter06`.

Understanding Functions

Azure Functions fills a large role in execution environments while focusing on event-based data processing. Traditionally, those environments have a lot of overhead in terms of hardware or **virtual machines** (**VMs**) and boilerplate code. Functions is Microsoft's execution environment to allow ease of development, deployment, and scaling. While a few types of underlying execution environments are available, it defaults to consumption, which brings a set of defaults that are well suited to a large variety of different data processing scenarios and are billed per event execution. If you need more CPU cores or memory, other environments are available; these will be covered later in this chapter. While all execution environments in Functions are considered serverless in the sense that you don't have to manage individual instances, other non-consumption environments are not pay-per-use and instead are charged based on the amount of CPU cores and memory allocated to each instance. C# is the predominant language that's used, although a variety of languages and bindings are supported.

The main entry points for the execution of these applications are triggers. A variety of these triggers exist to react to external events. From queue polling to ServiceBus pushing, reacting to blob, or database record changes, many ready-to-go bindings allow you to mix and match your solution. For APIs, the triggers we care most about are HTTP triggers.

HTTP triggers are exactly what they sound like: a request-response to a normal API request. These requests can come from all the usual suspects: browsers, webhooks, service-to-service calls, and so on. They can be routed to individual functions using the built-in routing template support. Incoming data from these routes can be automatically matched to the specified data types, deserialized, and bound.

Built-in authorization is either none or API key-based, with the latter available in two flavors: function-specific or a single global application key. Other standard authorization can be implemented with Entra ID, manually in code, or both.

Hosting should also be considered since your application will need to run somewhere – likely, though not necessarily, in the cloud. Various hosting and packaging options are provided, allowing you to tailor deployment to accommodate your application's needs. ZIP files, Docker, plain file copy (xcopy), and on-premises are all available. AMD64 Windows and Linux are supported on Azure, while ARM64 is supported in other scenarios.

At this point, you should have a good understanding of the environment in which Azure Functions operates and what's available to you.

Hosting

There are a variety of hosting options available to suit practically any need. Each has its pros and cons. **Consumption** is the default and will be used in this chapter. **Flex Consumption** (in preview at the time of writing), **Premium**, **Application Service Environment** (**ASE**), and **Kubernetes** are additional supported offerings that won't be discussed in this book.

Although powerful, Consumption comes with several limitations. First, the instance memory is limited to 1.5 GB, which can put a hard limit on the types of applications that can be run directly inside this Functions option. The second is that the instance only has a single core. The third is timeout. Azure only allows a timeout limit of 5 to 10 minutes.

However, many workloads do fit well within these constraints. From standard **Software-as-a-Service** (**SaaS**), APIs, and periodic updates to CRUD and Durable Functions-related calls (explained in the next chapter), the potential is there for the vast majority of these to fit well within the limits.

Needing more compute resources can be common in artificial intelligence workloads, for example. While Consumption is conceptually easy to think about, Premium is the next step up. You're billed for individual CPU vCores and GBs of memory allocated together in classic VM form. Managing these VMs is completely delegated to Azure. You set the maximum (and/or minimum) of the number of instances that the application can scale out to, and Azure handles the rest. The current limitations are 4 vCores and 14 GB of memory per host. Windows allows up to 100 hosts, and Linux between 20 and 100 hosts.

Application packaging

There are a few application packaging and deployment options available as well, depending on what size of resource you require. Docker is supported on Premium and App Service, allowing you to control the runtime environment with precision. ZIP files (published archives containing your entire application) are supported for all runtimes and required with Consumption.

History

Note that most of the runtime hosting modes, while they may still be available, are now considered deprecated. Originally, compiled functions were loaded inside the same physical operating system process that the function host was running in. This "in-proc" model allowed direct function calling between the host and custom functions but introduced potential issues with library dependencies and language updates. Hard dependencies on specific library versions couldn't be changed, and new C# language versions couldn't be used if they were incompatible with the existing runtime. Assembly loading quirks were also common, with varying success in workarounds.

Azure Functions initially launched with an Azure-based browser editor, and although it was serverless, the model had room for improvement. Later, a new version allowed standard .NET assemblies to be compiled so that the function host, starting the physical operating system process, would load. This introduced dependency resolution conflicts and required pinning functions to the same runtime version as the host, highlighting the need for further solutions.

Today, with out-of-process hosting, the majority of the aforementioned problems go away. Your function application runs in its own operating system process, managing its own startup, dependency injection, language, and .NET version. Communication is handled through an internal channel between the host application and your function application. This is the recommended way forward for .NET 6 and .NET 8 functions.

Though historical context is worth knowing for completeness, the defaults guide you through the recommended experience out of the box. So, how does the Consumption plan measure the usage of your API? Let's take a look.

Billing

The billing model for Consumption is a new metric that you may not be familiar with unless you've dealt with cloud cost estimation before. **Gigabytes per second** (**GB/s**) is the measure that's used in Consumption to accurately bill for applications and is the first part of the billing process. Whether they're quick and fast responses or memory-hungry multi-second responses, this style of metric allows it to be reported as a single numeric value. For example, a single request that takes 1 second to respond, using 1 GB of memory, would result in `1*1s*1GB=1GB/s` for billing. As for the inverse, four requests taking 250 milliseconds using the same 1 GB of memory would also equal 1 GB/s: `4*250ms*1GB=1GB/s`. At the time of writing, Azure's free tier grants 400,000 GB/s of free usage per month. With each request potentially taking an average of 100ms and using 256 MB of memory, that works out to be 16 million requests. The second part of billing is more straightforward: the number of requests. Azure grants 1 million requests for free per month, and it's $0.20 per million requests after that.

Project walkthrough

In this section, we'll begin creating a new Functions project, adding an additional HTTP trigger with an API route, and setting up some configuration that practically all applications will require.

Starting up

Creating a new Functions project is just like creating any other project. There are templates available in Visual Studio's new project wizard to aid you with this. Follow these steps:

1.   Select **Azure Functions** or search for it using the `functions` keyword and click **Next**:

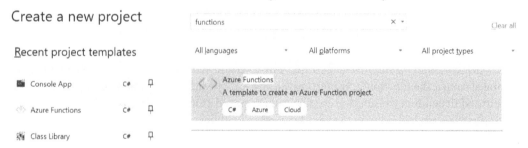

Figure 6.1 – New project wizard

2. Name your project and click **Next**:

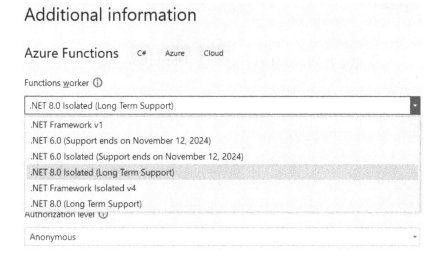

Figure 6.2 – Project configuration

3. Select the runtime and hosting configuration options. Usually, the latest **Long Term Support** option is a safe bet:

Figure 6.3 – Functions worker configuration

4. Select the **Http trigger** option, choose **Anonymous** under **Authorization level**, and click **Create**.

We'll cover authentication and authorization later in this book. As mentioned earlier, Docker containers are supported, but leave this option unchecked for now. Ensure the **Azurite** option is selected. This supports backend state management for various things and is also the "Durable" in Durable Functions, something that will be covered in the next chapter. Other triggers can be added later:

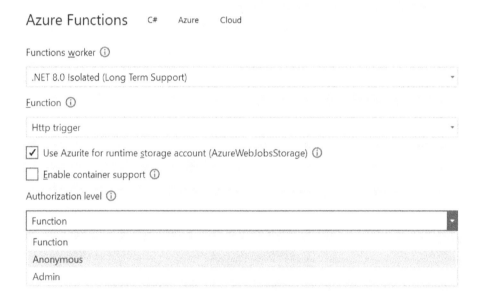

Figure 6.4 – Additional Functions authorization options

5. Many different triggers are available, and you can mix and match as needed. Right-click on the project in the **Solution Explorer** area and select **Add | New Azure Function**:

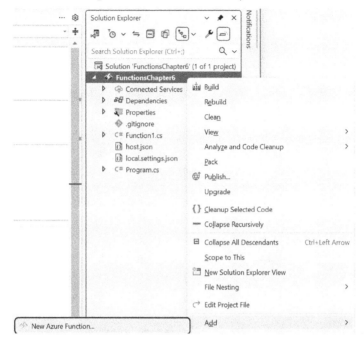

Figure 6.5 – Adding a new Azure Function

6. You may need to search for Function in the list, then click **Add**:

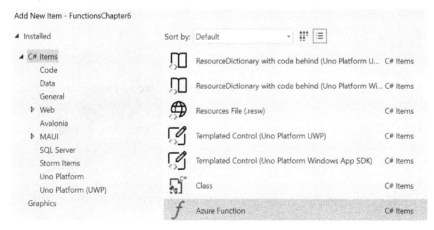

Figure 6.6 – New item dialog

7.   A list of triggers should appear. Select **Http trigger**, choose **Anonymous** for **Authorization level**, and click **Add**:

New Azure Function - Function

Figure 6.7 – The New Azure Function dialog

Note that templates are revised over time, and this new one may look different compared to the original Function. It also may add some interesting new objects that may look familiar to you, including `IActionResult` and `OkObjectResult`. These come from ASP.NET Core libraries. Install the latest `Microsoft.Azure.Functions.Worker.Extensions.Http.AspNetCore` NuGet package if it wasn't referenced by default.

With that, you've created two HTTP endpoints that should compile.

Options

Most applications will need options or configuration in some form. .NET provides built-in support for passing options in many forms, including custom ones, to your application when it starts up. These different instances, such as environment variables, JSON (`appsettings.json`) and XML files, and command-line arguments, are all layered on top of one another so that individual settings can be overridden as needed. Note that this is different from settings that are altered while the application is running, which are more advanced and circumstantial when creating APIs, and thus won't be covered in this book.

To add support for these options, follow these steps:

1.   Add a new class called `MyOptions`, make it `public`, and add a standard `string` property called `MyReturnValue`. We'll use this to control the return value of the Function.

2.   Go ahead and default the property value in the `MyOptions` class to anything you like. We'll override it in the `appsettings.json` file in a moment, and change it at startup time during deployment later in this chapter.

3.   Add a new property to the `appsettings.json` file named `MyReturnValue`, and a different value than you originally defaulted to in the code.

Now, we must configure the application so that it can use the configuration framework at startup.

4. Modify .ConfigureServices in Program.cs to add an additional argument to the context Lambda. Add calls to .AddOptions<MyOptions> to the services variable, or chain them onto the end of .ConfigureFunctionsApplicationInsights. Chain a call after .AddOptions to .BindConfiguration, taking an empty string. This binds values in the root configuration path to matching property names in the MyOptions class.

The Program.cs file should look this:

```
var host = new HostBuilder()
    .ConfigureFunctionsWebApplication()
    .ConfigureServices((context, services) =>
    {
        services.AddApplicationInsightsTelemetryWorkerService()
            .ConfigureFunctionsApplicationInsights()
            .AddOptions<MyOptions>()
            .BindConfiguration("");
    })
    .Build();
host.Run();
```

The MyOptions.cs file should look like this:

```
public class MyOptions
{
    public string? MyReturnProperty { get; set; } = "my value in
    code";
}
```

5. Modify Function1.cs so that it includes IOptions<MyOptions> in the constructor, then save a reference to that as a class member. Have OkObjectResult return _options. Value.MyReturnProperty so that we can see values changing.

The Function1.cs file should look like this:

```
public class Function1
{
    private readonly IOptions<MyOptions> _options;
    private readonly ILogger<Function1> _logger;

    public Function1(IOptions<MyOptions> options, ILogger<Function1>
    logger)
    {
        _options = options;
        _logger = logger;
    }


    [Function("Function1")]
    public IActionResult Run([HttpTrigger(AuthorizationLevel.
```

```
    Anonymous, "get", "post")] HttpRequest req)
    {
        _logger.LogInformation("C# HTTP trigger function processed a
        request.");
        return new OkObjectResult(_options.Value.MyReturnProperty);
    }
}
```

Test this out by running it. You should see the standard output console window with some informational Function messages including the visible routes. Hold *Ctrl* and click (on Windows) to run them in your browser, or use any standard HTTP software. You should see your hard-coded string as output:

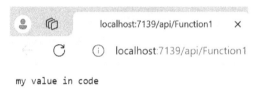

Figure 6.8 – Expected output in the browser

Congratulations! Not only is your Function running, but it's been set up so that its values can be altered at deployment time. Now, let's learn how to route incoming requests to different sections of code.

Routing

You'll almost certainly need multiple routes in your Function API, including routing parameters, query parameters, and so on. This forms part of the "shape" or public contract of your API. Routing supports this concept. If you're familiar with ASP.NET Core routes, then you'll be right at home as they're also supported, including constraints.

How do different requests know where to enter into your application? How should you describe what types of data should be allowed to be processed? Let's start with a classic storefront products endpoint:

1. Duplicate Function1.cs and rename it Products.cs, ensuring that you include all the references to Function1 in it.

2. Add string category and an int id parameter to the Run method.

3. Instead of returning a string in OkObjectResult, return an anonymous object containing category and id so that we can see the values that are passed in from the route.

The Product.cs file should look like this:

```
public class Products
{
    private readonly IOptions<MyOptions> _options;
```

```
    private readonly ILogger<Products> _logger;

    public Products(IOptions<MyOptions> options, ILogger<Products>
    logger)
    {
        _options = options;
        _logger = logger;
    }


    [Function(nameof(Products))]
    public IActionResult Run([HttpTrigger(AuthorizationLevel.
    Anonymous, "get", Route = "products/{category:alpha}/{id:int?}")]
    HttpRequest req,
        string category, int id = 0)
    {
        _logger.LogInformation("C# HTTP trigger function processed a
        request.");
        return new OkObjectResult(new
        {
            category,
            id
        });
    }
}
```

Note the new `Route` property in the `HttpTrigger` attribute, `"products/{category:alpha}/{id:int?}"`. This allows us to customize, restrict, and parse out the arguments from the desired endpoint. Since these route designs will likely be part of a larger web API for third-party consumers to use, you'll want to take care in creating them. You know that the product ID must be numeric, but you may want to restrict the category so that it only contains letters. When implemented as a route template, it would look like the one we mentioned previously: `"products/{category:alpha}/{id:int?}"`. This will only match incoming requests that have your desired URI segments in the specified format. The question mark (`?`) denotes that the specified parameter is optional, and can be defaulted in the method parameters.

Did you notice that *Figure 6.8* had the `api` URL segment prefixed to it when it wasn't specified in the route? Where does this prefix come from? By default, `api` is the default prefix for Functions. This can be changed in the `host.json` file under the `extensions` > `http` > `routePrefix` setting:

```
{
  "version": "2.0",
  "logging": {
    "applicationInsights": {
      "samplingSettings": {
```

```
        "isEnabled": true,
        "excludedTypes": "Request"
      },
      "enableLiveMetricsFilters": true
    }
  },
  "extensions": {
    "http": {
      "routePrefix": "myapi"
    }
  }
}
```

More details on overriding settings after deployment can be found in the *Post-deployment reconfiguration* section.

Now, let's create the necessary Azure cloud resources and environment.

Deploying

First, we need to create some resources before we can view them in Visual Studio.

Azure resource creation

Let's deploy your Function to production! To do so, create a new **Consumption Linux Function** and follow these steps:

1. Go to https://portal.azure.com and create a new resource group if you don't have one already:

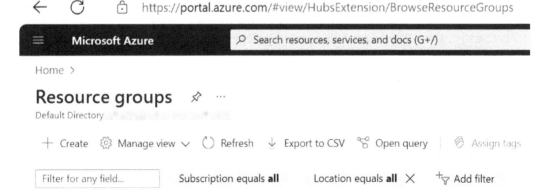

Figure 6.9 – Creating a new resource group

Place it in an Azure region geographically close to you. We'll use this same region when we create other resources to minimize lag and potential bandwidth. Click on the **Review + create** tab, then **Create**:

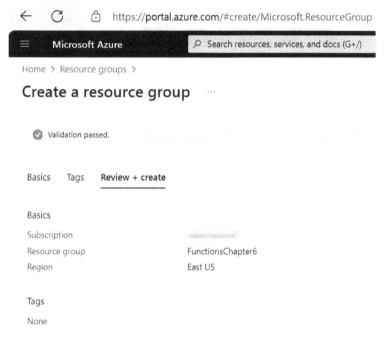

Figure 6.10 – Successfully creating a new resource group

2.   Inside this resource group, create a new Function app:

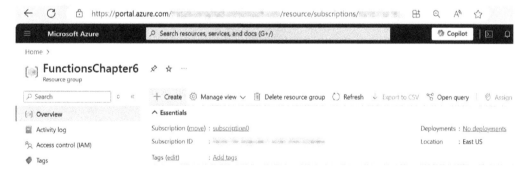

Figure 6.11 – Creating a new resource inside the resource group

3. Search for `function` if you don't see it in the default selection. Select **Create | Function App** to continue:

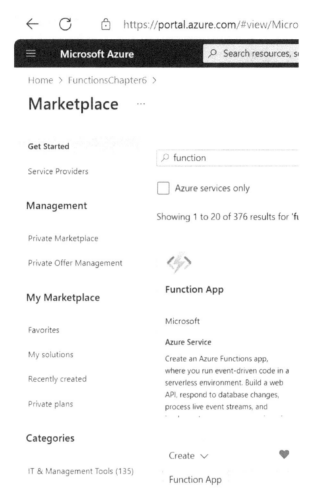

Figure 6.12 – Selecting Function App as the resource to create

4.   Next, select **Consumption** as your hosting option:

Figure 6.13 – Function hosting configuration

5. Select **.NET** for **Runtime stack**, **8 (LTS), isolated worker model** for **Version**, and **Linux** for **Operating system**. Select the region that you selected when you created the resource group and click **Next**:

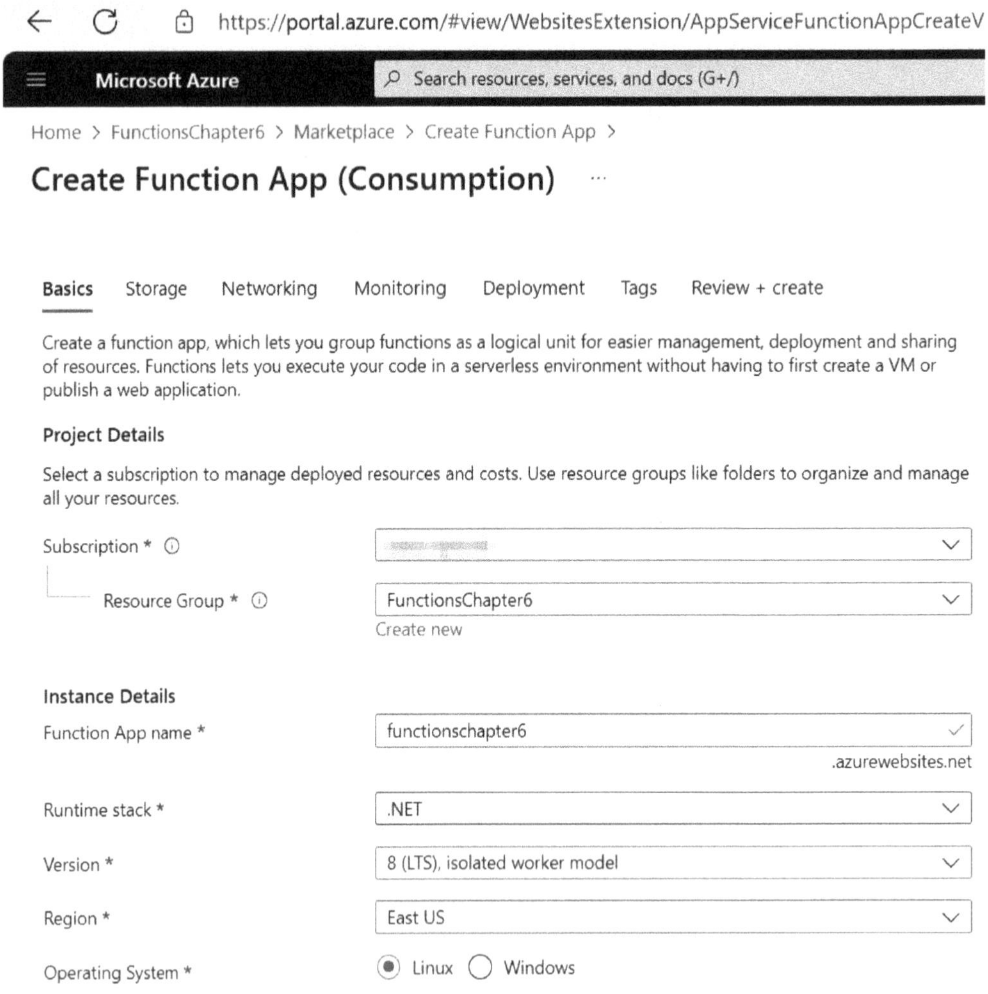

Figure 6.14 – Function details

6. A **storage account** resource will also need to be created to hold various things for the Function runtime, including logs, your deployment package, and optionally the Durable state, something we'll discuss in the next chapter. Disable **Blob service diagnostic settings** for now:

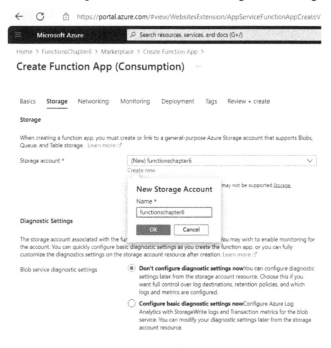

Figure 6.15 – Storage configuration

7. Enable **public access**. Then, choose **No** for **Enable Application Insights**:

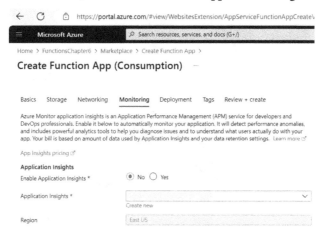

Figure 6.16 – Application Insights creation

8. Disable **continuous deployment**, an aspect that will also be covered in *Chapter 10*. We can use **Tags** to filter or group resources, and so on. Add tags if desired, or leave this section empty and click **Review + create**. Review your settings; if everything looks good, click **Create**.

9. At this point, the deployment process will continue. Click **Go to resource**; you'll be taken to your brand new Function!

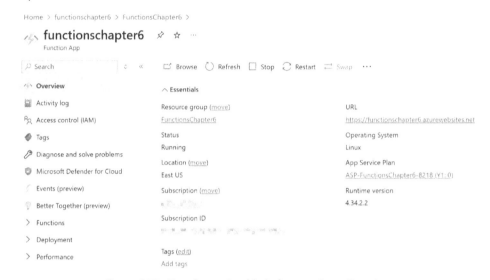

Figure 6.17 – Portal overview blade for your Azure Function

10. Click on the URL listed on the right-hand side. You'll be taken to a default page indicating that your Function is running:

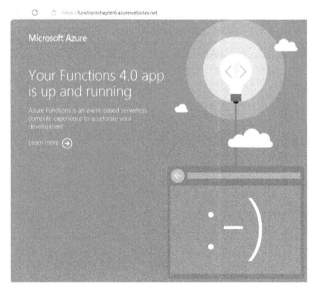

Figure 6.18 – Default Azure Functions landing page

> **Tip**
>
> While these steps and screenshots are accurate at the time of writing, Azure often changes and upgrades its design, features, flow, and so on. It's recommended that you check out the official documentation for updated guidance.

Now that the Function resource is running with a default template, let's deploy from Visual Studio.

Publishing from Visual Studio

Let's walk through deploying manually from Visual Studio. Automated deployments, also known as continuous delivery, will be covered in *Chapter 10*:

1. Back in **Visual Studio**, right-click on the **FunctionsChapter6** project and select **Publish…**:

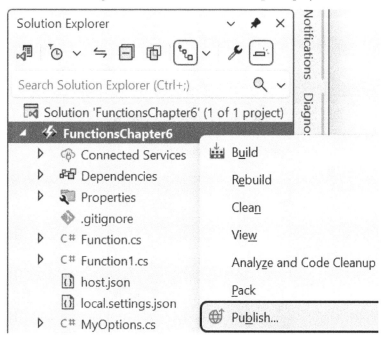

Figure 6.19 – Publishing our project

2. Then, select **Azure** and click **Next**:

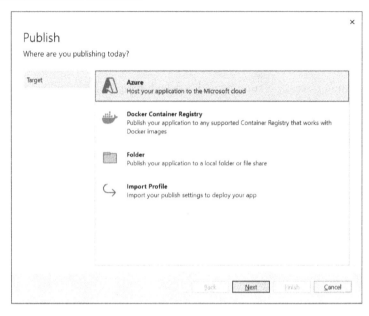

Figure 6.20 – Types of publishing

3. Select **Azure Function App (Linux)** and click **Next**:

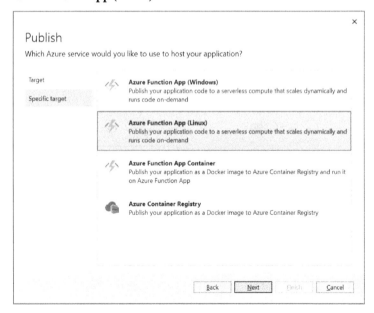

Figure 6.21 – Azure publishing targets

4. Select the **Microsoft account** and **subscription** you created the Function resource under. Search or locate your Function by name, select it, and click **Finish**:

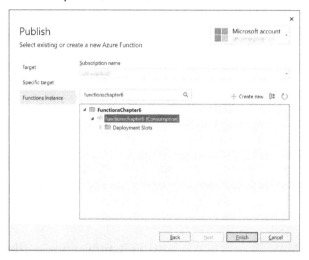

Figure 6.22 – Selecting the account, subscription, and resource to publish to

5. Click **Finish**, then **Close** when you're done. Details about your published profile will appear, including its **Configuration** and **Target Runtime**, as well as any dependencies that it needs:

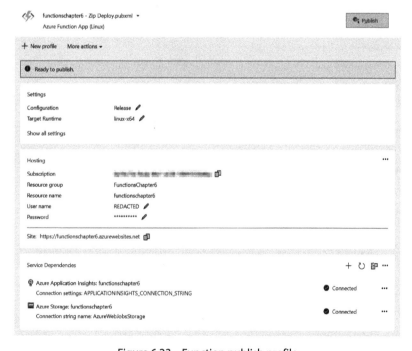

Figure 6.23 – Function publish profile

When you're ready, click **Publish**. Once that succeeds, you can view your new API route at `https://<my resource name>.azurewebsites.net/api/products/electronics/471337`. Note that you can see the default data if you go to `https://<my resource name>.azurewebsites.net/api/Function`.

As mentioned previously in this chapter, we'll now look at changing a configuration value without recompiling the Function, and without redeploying it.

Post-deployment reconfiguration

Now, let's change the configuration to a different value:

1. In the **Environment variables** blade, under the **Settings** section of the Function resource in the Azure portal, create a new key to override the setting we hard-coded earlier. Use `MyReturnProperty` as the key since we're reading the configuration variables from the root namespace:

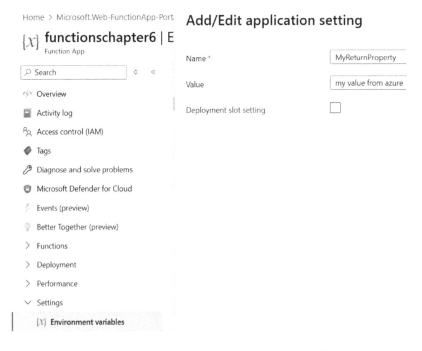

Figure 6.24 - Adding a new environment variable to override a setting

2. **Apply** this addition, **Apply** the changes, and **Confirm** the save; your Function application will be restarted. Navigate to `https://<my resource name>.azurewebsites.net/api/Function1` so that you can see the new configuration value:

← → C   🔒 https://functionschapter6.azurewebsites.net/api/Function1

my value from azure

Figure 6.25 – Overridden configuration value

This can be nested arbitrarily deep. For example, if your `MyOptions` class's `MyReturnValue` was a complex type with its own `MyOtherReturnValue` property, the path for the key in Azure would be `MyReturnValue__MyOtherReturnValue`. Note that there are two underscores between the property names.

Since this is publicly accessible, it has the potential to cost you money if a rogue process becomes aware of your new endpoint. Securing this new site with what's colloquially known as **Easy Auth** will be discussed later in this book.

But in the meantime, you can adjust some hosting options to limit the potential cost.

1. Navigate to **Settings | Scale out** and change **Maximum Scale Out Limit** to **1**. Then, click **Save**:

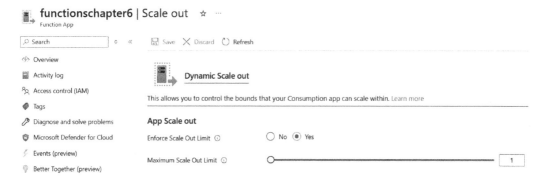

Figure 6.26 – Limiting scale out

2. Then, navigate to **Settings | Configuration**, change **Daily Usage Quota** to **1**, and click **Save**, then **Continue**:

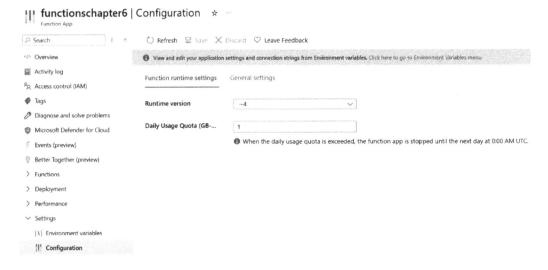

Figure 6.27 – Adding a daily quota

At this point, while you haven't secured your site against bots or malicious actors, you have at least taken a few steps to mitigate any potential damage.

Summary

In this chapter, we walked through creating multiple HTTP endpoints inside a single Azure Function, adding a route template to assist with managing differing URI segments at runtime. Then, we added configuration options to our project, deployed it to Azure, and adjusted the configuration options after deployment. To limit the potential cost of a deployed, live HTTP endpoint, we adjusted two settings until authorization was in place.

Now that you understand how HTTP triggers work in Azure Functions, in the next chapter, we'll explore other types of triggers we can use to build reliable, stateful, and scalable workflows.

You try it

Write an API using Azure Functions, create a Function resource in Azure, and then deploy your Function to it with Visual Studio.

7

Azure Durable Functions

In the previous chapter, we discussed how HTTP APIs in Azure Functions provide an alternative hosting model, as well as solve many traditional problems associated with manual hosting.

Do you need to massively parallelize hundreds of millions of tasks on an arbitrary number of physical processes or nodes (fan-out) and then wait for them all to complete (fan-in)? Do you then need the app to wait for a human or other process to review and take action to continue the next step? What if that human is unavailable and you need to *timeout* the review process instead? This situation of events is easily expressible in code, and we'll be tackling a subset of this scenario in this chapter.

In this chapter, we will look at the following:

- Expanding on standard APIs to create resilient, stateful workflows
- Differences in debugging these workflows compared to previous chapters
- Interacting and injecting data into live systems using standard HTTP APIs
- Briefly discussing how to set up other common usage patterns

Technical requirements

Building Azure Durable Functions in Visual Studio has the same requirements as for *Chapter 6*. The source code for this chapter is available at `https://github.com/PacktPublishing/Programming-APIs-with-C-Sharp-and-.NET/tree/main/Chapter07`.

Overview of Durable Functions

Durable Functions gets its very descriptive name from what it does under the hood: save its state to persistent storage in case of crashes, outages, dependency problems, and so on. Not only does this allow for problems to be recovered from easily but it also allows scalability and coordination among tasks. Durability in an Azure function is provided using a standard storage account by default. Tables, blobs, and queues are all used under the hood:

- Tables are used for managing function execution history, including parameters and return values

- Blob storage is used for the automatic storage of large parameters passed to activities
- Queues are used for triggering activities and orchestration instances

SQL Server and Netherite are the other two supported durable store options that are not covered in this book but can be used in advanced scenarios.

While there is never an "easy button" for scaling in a distributed system, the following two specific rules simplify an enormous amount of platform- and dependency-related overhead, allowing you to focus on the logic of the code itself:

- Orchestrator functions must be deterministic
- Activity functions must be idempotent

Orchestrator functions are exactly what they sound like: they orchestrate, or control the execution order of, activities, which usually contain the bulk of the work or logic of the application. A major restriction that must be followed with orchestrators is that they must be deterministic, which also means that they cannot do any form of I/O directly. All activity, sub-orchestrator, or other awaited calls must be in the same order to return the executing code to its exact state just prior to the next `await` call. Other nondeterministic APIs that you must be aware of fall into categories such as DateTimes, GUIDs, I/O, and other async APIs. In general, if you need data from outside the durable context, use activities to retrieve it.

Activity functions are always called by orchestrators, and cannot be called directly from anything else. These are where the bulk of the application logic usually happens, and compared to orchestrators, activity functions have one restriction: they must be idempotent. There is no guarantee that an activity instance will run exactly once, so be sure that multiple runs in succession have the same result.

Adding durable support to your existing function is as easy as adding a NuGet package. All the functions, triggers, and so on can interoperate and coexist in a single project, depending on your application requirements.

Before Durable Functions, in a manually written situation with only basic OS platform support, you had to manage the state yourself. This included handling crashes, and marking tasks as done, errored, in progress, and so on. Restarts also had to be managed, as did advanced processing such as a parallel fan-out situation. Using Durable Functions simplifies all these requirements.

Now, let's look at starting up a durable instance, and how these objects coordinate tasks in a stateful system.

Orchestrators

The main "entry point" into the Durable system is through an orchestrator. These are started up inside the running function using `DurableTaskClient`, or outside of a function process by using the HTTP management APIs discussed later in the *Programming and debugging walk-through* section. I say *entry point* because I find it conceptually easier to think about it in this way. While the OS process itself still uses the classic `Task` or void `Main(...)`, data or message processing in a Durable system usually begins with a method marked with a `Function` attribute, and `DurableTaskClient` marked with an `OrchestrationTrigger` attribute.

Serializable data objects, usually in JSON form, can be passed into the orchestrator when an instance is created. These can be things such as larger descriptive objects, SAS tokens to blob storage, binary data that must be deserialized, or all of them combined. While you can work with standard strings or `JsonNodes` (sometimes you must), my preferred way is to use the generic method overloads and create serialization classes to mirror the structure of the data being passed around in the system. This ensures that it is easy to modify the objects over time, delegating the type-checking to the compiler. This also sidesteps a runtime issue that sometimes occurs during development: missing or mismatched serialization classes, which are not immediately apparent as there would be no standard compilation errors or runtime exceptions. The same will apply to activities.

Since orchestration instances are durable and their state is written to persistent storage, this means that a running orchestration instance does not need to stay loaded into RAM while it waits for an activity to finish. Taking this a step further, it need not resume running on the same OS process, virtual machine, or physical machine. This can lead to highly performant and efficient allocation of compute and memory resources. In the extreme case, you could have hundreds or thousands of orchestration instances awaiting future completion of tasks, all without using compute or memory, only minimal storage.

Continuing to take this further, you could have an infinite loop that also does not use any compute or memory while awaiting a task. This concept, called an eternal orchestrator, could respond to outside events, act, and durably wait until the next event. A small caveat though: since orchestration instances save their history to rebuild their state in the future, an eternal orchestrator could have an ever-growing history, which would eventually cause performance problems. A method called `ContinueAsNew` truncates that history, which prevents it from growing.

With any API or stateful workflow, you'll almost certainly need to process something, make network calls, and so on. Since we are unable to do so in orchestrators, this is where activities come in.

Activities

The pieces of code that actually contain most of your logic are activities. They have one very specific requirement: they must be idempotent. This means your code must have no side effects if it happens to execute more than once, as there is no guarantee that a specific instance will execute exactly once. Due to various reasons, some out of your control, activities may be terminated in the middle of execution. This must be handled in your activity code so that when the Durable system detects an incomplete instance, starting from the beginning is not a problem.

Various built-in programming constructs that you would normally not think about, now have a profound potential impact on the rest of the system. For example, `Guid.NewGuid()` should likely not be used in an activity. Creating files, saving database records, or calling other APIs with this random GUID could now result in an orphaned record if the activity needed to be restarted from the beginning. Instead, you could create the new GUID inside the orchestrator, and pass that into the activity with its object parameter. The `TaskOrchestrationContext` instance passed into the orchestrator has a specific method called `NewGuid` to facilitate this exact need.

Programming and debugging walk-through

Using the existing *Chapter 6* function code, let's add support for Durable to it. Right-click on the project and select **Add | New Azure Function** just as you did with the first HTTP endpoint. Give it a name, and then select **Durable Functions Orchestration**.

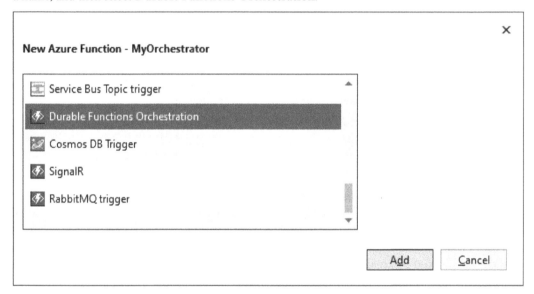

Figure 7.1 – Adding a new Durable Functions orchestration

You can see from the provided template that three static methods were created corresponding to each of the concepts we discussed earlier: a regular function with `HttpTrigger`, which schedules a new orchestration instance to run, which then calls one or more activities. Visual Studio should have added a reference to `Microsoft.Azure.Functions.Worker.Extensions.DurableTask` automatically, but add it via NuGet if it did not.

> **Note**
>
> Notice that these methods are all static. Though this does work, it leaves a lot to be desired as it prevents impactful concepts discussed in the last chapter such as options, dependency injection, and easier testing. Durable Functions also supports migrating the code to the non-static style in the previous chapter. This exercise is left up to you. We are using the word "the" when referring to the orchestrator and activity we are working on. This may seem out of place since we are referring to single static methods and not necessarily an object or thing you can see visually. The same static method may also be executing in different threads, processes, and virtual machines concurrently with different data. If you do decide to undertake the code migration, the individual files with regular constructors and non-static methods may help you conceptually visualize them.

We'll focus on saving some data to a file and waiting for an event that will then update the file again. Let's begin by deleting the contents of the SayHello method, which contains a string parameter, name, with ActivityTrigger on it. This is your one and only parameter that can be passed to your activity from your orchestrator. Though this can be a string, generally, it is some kind of data transfer or **Plain Old C# Class** (**POCO**) object that must be JSON serializable. The FunctionContext executionContext parameter can be used to discover information about the running activity, among other things. Change the return type to Task<string>, and add a line that awaits a call to File.WriteAllTextAsync, giving it a filename of your choosing, and then the contents will be the name string parameter marked with ActivityTrigger. Rename this parameter and its references to contents by pressing *F2*. This activity is simple and straightforward, which will add extra value to the orchestrator when we use it more than once.

The SayHello method should resemble this:

```
[Function(nameof(SayHello))]
public static async Task<string> SayHello([ActivityTrigger] string
contents, FunctionContext executionContext)
{
    await File.WriteAllTextAsync("myfile.txt", contents);
    return default;
}
```

In the RunOrchestrator method, delete the contents and add an awaited call to context. CallActivityAsync, passing it the name of the activity, which, in our case, is SayHello. Change the return to Task<object> and then return default to make the compiler happy. Add an awaited call to context.WaitForExternalEvent<ExpandoObject>("MyEvent") after that, and save that into a dynamic variable. Finally, let's add another call to our first activity, but this time, pass it the dynamic awaited event's value property that we received from the external event call.

> **Tip**
>
> Though you can use a normal double-quoted string when calling an activity via `CallActivityAsync`, using the `nameof` expression is particularly powerful here as it not only evaluates to a string during compile time but also responds to symbol renaming. We'll use this in the sample. The same idea can be used for `WaitForExternalEvent` by using the POCO class name, for example.

The `RunOrchestrator` method should resemble this:

```
[Function(nameof(MyOrchestrator))]
public static async Task<object> RunOrchestrator(
    [OrchestrationTrigger] TaskOrchestrationContext context)
{
    await context.CallActivityAsync(nameof(SayHello)
);
    dynamic eventValue = await context.
    WaitForExternalEvent<ExpandoObject>("MyEvent");
    await context.CallActivityAsync(nameof(SayHello)
    , eventValue.value);
    return default;
}
```

> **Tip**
>
> The `Function` runtime mandates that we pass JSON data to this endpoint, which would then be automatically deserialized and returned from our awaited `WaitForExternalEvent` call. This ensures a baseline level of backward compatibility in case things need to change in the future. For our testing purposes, we are using `dynamic` to reduce the number of boilerplate files that would need to be created during this chapter.

Let's start debugging in Visual Studio, and *Ctrl*/*CMD* click on the `MyOrchestrator_HttpStart` HTTP trigger to run our orchestrator entrypoint. Navigate to the output folder on the function, likely in `bin/debug/net8.0`, and notice there's an empty file. This is the result of the first call to the `SayHello` activity. What is the function doing now? It is currently awaiting the call to `WaitForExternalEvent`. Copy or save the URI specified by the `sendEventPostUri` element, as we'll need that in a moment. Let's stop debugging now so that the physical application process terminates. Immediately start debugging again, but do not click on the link again to start a new instance. Our previous instance is still "running" in the Durable Functions sense, only it is not taking up memory, CPU, or any other OS resource, except for storage space.

Open up your favorite REST client interface such as the new built-in one from Visual Studio, Postman, and so on. You'll need the URI you copied previously to signal our running orchestration instance event. We'll be using Visual Studio. Create a new text file by right-clicking on the project, selecting **Add | New Item…**, and then selecting **Text File**. The name of this file should end with .http so that Visual Studio recognizes it. Type POST in all uppercase, and then paste in the URI that you copied earlier. Replace {eventName} with the name that you chose in the code; we used MyEvent. Add a header with the Content-Type: application/json value so that the Function runtime accepts it. Ensure that there is an empty line after the URI, then type some valid JSON with a value property and value. To end the body of the request, make sure that there is also an empty line afterward.

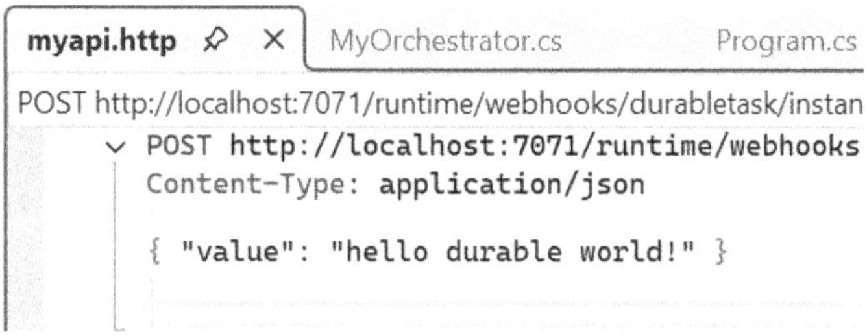

```
myapi.http  ⚲  ✕    MyOrchestrator.cs         Program.cs

POST http://localhost:7071/runtime/webhooks/durabletask/instan
      ∨ POST http://localhost:7071/runtime/webhooks
        Content-Type: application/json

        { "value": "hello durable world!" }
```

Figure 7.2 – REST client setup in Visual Studio

Switch to the orchestrator file and place a breakpoint on both calls to our activity. Send the POST request using the Send request link in the .http file. The first breakpoint should now hit. But wait, why was the first one hit when we already ran this line and are waiting on the line after that? Hover over the context variable and expand it to look at the read-only IsReplaying property. Notice that it is true.

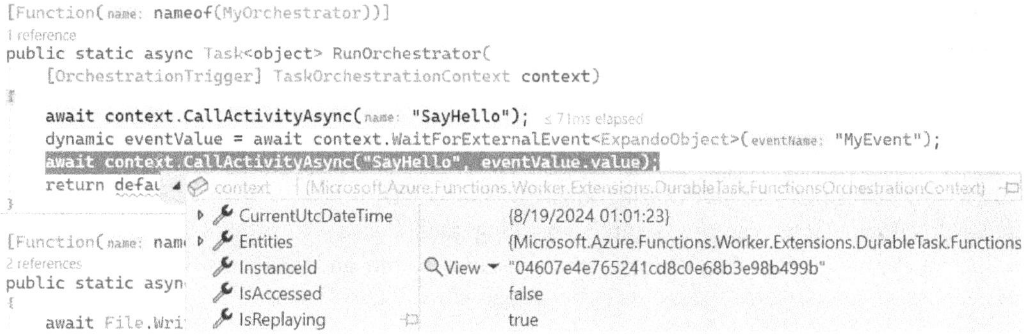

```
[Function( name: nameof(MyOrchestrator))]
1 reference
public static async Task<object> RunOrchestrator(
    [OrchestrationTrigger] TaskOrchestrationContext context)
{
    await context.CallActivityAsync( name: "SayHello");  ≤ 71ms elapsed
    dynamic eventValue = await context.WaitForExternalEvent<ExpandoObject>( eventName: "MyEvent");
    await context.CallActivityAsync("SayHello", eventValue.value);
    return defau  ▲ ⊗ context   | (Microsoft.Azure.Functions.Worker.Extensions.DurableTask.FunctionsOrchestrationContext) ⊡
}
                        ▶ ⚿ CurrentUtcDateTime        {8/19/2024 01:01:23}
[Function( name: nam  ▶ ⚿ Entities               {Microsoft.Azure.Functions.Worker.Extensions.DurableTask.Functions
2 references               ⚿ InstanceId       �🔍View ▾ "04607e4e765241cd8c0e68b3e98b499b"
public static asyn        ⚿ IsAccessed            false
{                         ⚿ IsReplaying    ⊡      true
    await File.Wri
```

Figure 7.3 – IsReplaying is true

This is exactly what the property's name sounds like; it is quite literally rebuilding its internal state line by line. It will do this after every single `await`. This is why orchestrators must be deterministic so that the internal state is always exactly the same no matter how many times it must rerun the same logic over and over. Every single call to these `await` methods is saved in durable storage. At some point in the future, they are queried, deserialized, and returned to the calling orchestrator. Press *F10* to step over the first activity call, and check to see that the `IsReplaying` property is still `true`. Step again over `WaitForExternalEvent`, which should return immediately. Now, look at the `IsReplaying` property again; it should be `false`. This means it is the very first time that this code has been run for this orchestration instance.

```
[Function( name: nameof(MyOrchestrator))]
1 reference
public static async Task<object> RunOrchestrator(
    [OrchestrationTrigger] TaskOrchestrationContext context)
{
    await context.CallActivityAsync( name: "SayHello");
    dynamic eventValue = await context.WaitForExternalEvent<ExpandoObject>( eventName: "MyEvent");
    await context.CallActivityAsync("SayHello", eventValue.value);    ≤ 4ms elapsed
    return del ▲ ⊘ context    {Microsoft.Azure.Functions.Worker.Extensions.DurableTask.FunctionsOrchestrationContext}    ▭
}
                        ▶ 🔑 CurrentUtcDateTime         {8/19/2024 00:56:55}
[Function( name: n ▶ 🔑 Entities                {Microsoft.Azure.Functions.Worker.Extensions.DurableTask.Functions
2 references          🔑 InstanceId      🔍 View ▾ "d9ba5df0b72c458fba27f671336d91fa"
public static as     🔑 IsAccessed               true
{                    🔑 IsReplaying     ▭      false
    await File.W
```

Figure 7.4 – IsReplaying is false

Press *F5* to continue; it should immediately call the activity. Navigate to the output folder again and open the file. You should see the contents of the value property that you set in the `.http` file's POST request. The orchestration instance is now completed. If you query durable storage, you'll find the complete history of this orchestration instance, including all input and output parameters, errors if there are any, and timestamps. This will allow you to analyze the orchestration instance later if needed or for tracking, logging, and so on. We'll look at how to view this in a moment.

Waiting on activities, external events, and sub-orchestrators is powerful all on its own. However, we can take it one step further. Using the existing language features such as `List<Task>`, `Task.WhenAny`, or `Task.WhenAll`, we can have an arbitrarily long stateful execution system. This can scale, wait for potentially hundreds or thousands of activity instances to run, and then move on to the next code.

> **Tip**
> Using `Task.WhenAny`, we can wait on an external human event or a timeout. This allows us to default to an action if an external event is not received in time.

To have an easier time debugging, you're likely to want to be familiar with clearing the durable storage. This allows you to start from a clean state. If you have many outstanding orchestration instances, timers, and so on, it can be difficult when debugging anything in the same project. Using Azure Storage Explorer, navigate to **Emulator & Attached** | **(Emulator – Default Ports) (Key)** | **Tables**, and open two tables that end with `History` and `Instances`. Look around for a bit to see how the data is physically stored if interested. When done, right-click on the `History` table and select **Delete**. Do the same for `Instances`.

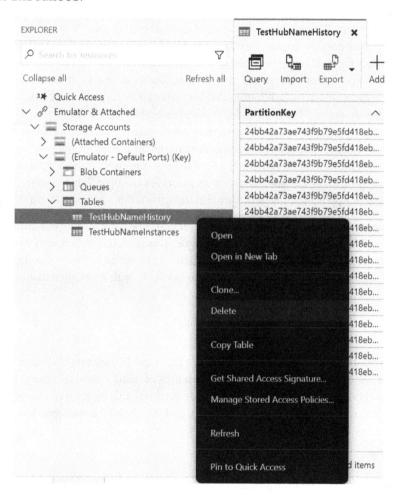

Figure 7.5 – Clearing the local History table

There are additional advanced topics not covered here. Some of them are durable entities, and a counterpart, critical sections (.NET only). These together let you coordinate distributed locks inside an orchestrator.

Additional options

Sometimes, you want an orchestrator to continuously wait for an external event without ever exiting. Using a standard `for` or `while` loop around the call to `WaitForExternalEvent` is reasonable for a low number of events. But recall how previously I mentioned that every single `await` is some type of network call to the durable storage. Having `await` inside of a loop has the potential to drastically increase the latency for building up the internal state. An alternative way to support this exact scenario is to use eternal orchestrations with a call to `ContinueAsNew`. Though these are especially suited for the situation described, it's worth noting that they have some considerations you need to keep in mind. While they do prevent the continuous growth of durable storage for that instance, they do so by truncating the history. This may be acceptable in your situation, but it could also not be. Note that while you have lost the underlying execution history in the durable store, nothing is preventing you from manually logging things that you need or want to keep. You could have a logging activity in place throughout your code to log various important events to, for example, Table storage. There's also the option of logging to Application Insights. However, Insights is not a permanent log storage solution.

Sometimes, you want a single instance of a global orchestrator throughout your entire application. These can be useful in background tasks, for example. This is accomplished with what is known as singleton orchestrators. It does not have a specific method call per se, but to enable this functionality, all you need to do is start an orchestration instance normally with a specified instance ID that will not change.

Exceptions

While most programming constructs are available, a bit of special care must be taken when working with exceptions. Using C#, we do have first-class handling of them. However, since this is potentially across a process boundary, a notable incompatibility is when catching derived exception types. You should, in general, catch the normal base exception, and then handle it appropriately.

Summary

In this chapter, we discussed how the durable orchestration system comprising activities and orchestrators helps to solve a wide variety of use cases. We then walked through adding Durable Functions to our existing Functions code from the previous chapter. Via debugging, we demonstrated how the orchestrator rebuilds its internal state, and how to get information into a running orchestration instance. We then discussed some helpful tips to clear the local durable store during development and touched on some additional features and pitfalls.

In the next chapter, we'll take a look at related concepts including Table storage, Aspire, and some additional advanced API topics.

You try it

Create or modify an existing HTTP trigger to start a new Orchestration instance. Have your new Orchestrator await at least two Activities (they can be the same one) so you can debug and step through to watch it rebuild its internal state. The Activity can be something minimal for this, a single API call to anywhere or something else. After it completes, view the Table Storage durable logs in Azure or Azure Storage Explorer. Examine how the logs in the history table line up with your orchestrator.

8

Advanced Topics

In this chapter, we will examine a few advanced topics not covered elsewhere in the book. This includes Implementing an Advanced API using a more complex data structure, Storage Tables, and the very exciting new (at the time of this writing) Aspire feature.

In this chapter, we will cover the following topics:

- Implementing an advanced API
- Updating the database
- Supporting implementation
- Creating Azure Storage Tables
- Aspire dashboard
- Adding Aspire to existing projects

Technical requirements

For this chapter, you'll need the following:

- Visual Studio.
- The `Azure.Data.Tables` NuGet package.
- An Azure account (you can get a free starter account at `https://azure.microsoft.com/en-us/`).

  Aspire comes with Visual Studio 2022 (version 17.10 or higher) and requires .NET 8.

- You will need to install Docker Desktop (which is free and can be obtained at `https://www.docker.com/Products/docker-desktop/`).

The code files for this chapter can be found in the GitHub repository here: `https://github.com/PacktPublishing/Programming-APIs-with-C-Sharp-and-.NET/tree/main/Chapter08`

Implementing an advanced API

Until now, we've been working with a very simple database, and implementing pretty straightforward APIs. From time to time, however, your client will ask for something more difficult or complex. Let's take a look at one such requirement.

The client has asked for the ability to see a car with all its options. We'll provide that in JSON for easy display on the web, phone, and so on. The JSON will look like this:

```json
{
    "id": 2,
    "name": "buick skylark 320",
    "mpg": null,
    "cylinders": null,
    "displacement": null,
    "horsepower": null,
    "weight": null,
    "acceleration": null,
    "modelYear": null,
    "origin": null,
    "is_Deleted": null,
    "options": [
        {
            "optionId": 1,
            "optionName": "Winter Package",
            "optionPrice": 3700
        },
        {
            "optionId": 2,
            "optionName": "Mats",
            "optionPrice": 250
        },
        {
            "optionId": 3,
            "optionName": "Summer Package",
            "optionPrice": 2250
        }
    ]
}
```

To implement this, we'll need to add a table to the database: Options.

Updating the database

We need to track various features (options) the user may select, such as a sunroof, the winter package, and so on. To do this, we will create a new table, Options, which will have four columns:

- car_id: The ID of the car to which this option will be added

- option_id: The ID of the option

- option_name: The name of the feature

- option_price: The MSRP for this feature

Here is a sample of the Options table:

	car_id	option_id	option_name	option_price
1	2	1	Winter Package	3700
2	5	1	Winter Package	3700
3	5	2	Mats	250
4	4	2	Mats	250
5	2	2	Mats	250
6	2	3	Summer Package	2250
7	5	3	Summer Package	2250
8	5	4	Speaker Upgrade	1275
9	5	5	Leather	8500

Figure 8.1 – Sample rows from the Options table

You'll want to create at least 10 rows using arbitrary values. Note that there is no table with the option names and values. This is a simple mostly non-relational database, though you are free to add such tables.

With this table, we can create our one relationship; that is between the car table and the Options table. Add car_id to the car table, and create our Select statement with a join to the options table:

```
select top(10) * from car c join options o on o.car_id = c.id
```

The result looks like the car table, but has the options for each car appended to the end, as shown in *Figure 8.2*:

	name	mpg	cylinders	displacement	id	car_id	option_id	option_name	option_price
1	buick skylark 320	15	8	350	2	2	1	Winter Package	3700
2	buick skylark 320	15	8	350	2	2	2	Mats	250
3	buick skylark 320	15	8	350	2	2	3	Summer Package	2250
4	subaru impreza	16	8	304	4	4	2	Mats	250
5	subaru forester	17	8	302	5	5	1	Winter Package	3700
6	subaru forester	17	8	302	5	5	2	Mats	250
7	subaru forester	17	8	302	5	5	3	Summer Package	2250
8	subaru forester	17	8	302	5	5	4	Speaker Upgrade	1275
9	subaru forester	17	8	302	5	5	5	Leather	8500

Figure 8.2 – Joined tables

Note that your table will look a bit different as I've cut out the middle to make it fit the page.

You can see that the option values are appended to the `car` rows. This is just what we need.

For most applications, this would be sufficient, however, our client has asked for the JSON structure shown in the code under the *Implementing an advanced API* heading.

This will be a bit tricky.

Creating the classes

We need a class to represent the entire row, with the car and the options together. Each instance of the class will represent one full row in the table, as shown in *Figure 8.2*. Let's call that class `CarFlat`:

```
public class CarFlat : Car
{
    public int? car_id { get; set; }
    public int? option_id { get; set; }
    public string? option_name { get; set; }
    public float option_price { get; set; }
}
```

Notice that `CarFlat` inherits from `Car`, picking up all the properties of `Car` and adding the properties of `Options` (along with `car_id`).

> **Note**
>
> In my programming, I typically use Pascal case (initial cap) for properties.

Now, we need a class to represent the row without the options (representing the car) but each car will have a collection of options. Let's call that class `CarDto` as it will be our **data transfer object** (**DTO**) for the car.

We will be passing options around, so let's create an `OptionsDto` class as well.

Here's what they look like:

```
public class CarDto
{
    public int Id { get; set; }
    public string Name { get; set; }
    public string Mpg { get; set; }
    public string Cylinders { get; set; }
    public string Displacement { get; set; }
    public string Horsepower { get; set; }
    public string Weight { get; set; }
```

```
        public string Acceleration { get; set; }
        public string ModelYear { get; set; }
        public string Origin { get; set; }
        public string Is_Deleted { get; set; }
        public List<OptionsDto> Options { get; set; }
    }
```

The important thing to note here is that CarDto has a property that is the list of all this car's options; notice that the final property is a list of OptionsDtos. Let's look at that class now:

Here is OptionsDto:

```
    public class OptionsDto
    {
        public int OptionId { get; set; }
        public string OptionName { get; set; }
        public float OptionPrice { get; set; }
    }
```

Notice the capitalization and absence of underscores in the DTO.

We need a way to link the DTO to the Car object. That is what profiles are for.

The profile

We'll need a profile to map the various classes to one another. The DTO is used to transfer the object (hence the name) but it must be mapped to the original object. Thus, we want to map Car.Dto to the Car class.

This is the trickiest part, and mapping is what makes this all work.

The first map is pretty straightforward, mapping the Car to CarDto:

```
CreateMap<CarDto, Car>()
    .ForMember(car => car.id, opt => opt.MapFrom(carDto => carDto.Id))
    .ForMember(car => car.name, opt => opt.MapFrom(carDto => carDto.
    Name))
    .ForMember(car => car.mpg, opt => opt.MapFrom(carDto => carDto.
    Mpg))
    .ForMember(car => car.cylinders, opt => opt.MapFrom(carDto =>
    carDto.Cylinders))
    .ForMember(car => car.displacement, opt => opt.MapFrom(carDto =>
    carDto.Displacement))
    .ForMember(car => car.horsepower, opt => opt.MapFrom(carDto =>
    carDto.Horsepower))
    .ForMember(car => car.weight, opt => opt.MapFrom(carDto => carDto.
```

```
        Weight))
    .ForMember(car => car.acceleration, opt => opt.MapFrom(carDto =>
    carDto.Acceleration))
    .ForMember(car => car.model_year, opt => opt.MapFrom(carDto =>
    carDto.ModelYear))
    .ForMember(car => car.origin, opt => opt.MapFrom(carDto => carDto.
    Origin))
    .ReverseMap();
```

We start by identifying the types in the map, and then for each member, we map using Lambda expressions. Note the last line, `.ReerseMap` – this saves us the trouble of re-writing the entire map going the other way.

Next comes the heart of the program, mapping `CarFlat` to `CarDto` and mapping `OptionsDto` to `CarFlat`:

```
CreateMap<List<CarFlat>, CarDto>()
    .ForPath(dest => dest.Id, opt => opt.MapFrom(src => src.First().
    id))
    .ForPath(dest => dest.Name, opt => opt.MapFrom(src => src.
    First().name))
    .ForMember(dest => dest.Options, opt => opt.MapFrom(src => src));

CreateMap<OptionsDto, CarFlat>()
    .ForMember(dest => dest.option_id, opt => opt.MapFrom(src => src.
    OptionId))
    .ForMember(dest => dest.option_name, opt => opt.MapFrom(src =>
    src.OptionName))
    .ForMember(dest => dest.option_price, opt => opt.MapFrom(src =>
    src.OptionPrice))
```

The magic is performed by AutoMapper. If you have not installed AutoMapper yet, this is a good time to do so. AutoMapper will make this job infinitely easier. AutoMapper simplifies the mapping process between different object models, reducing the need for manual transformations. All we need to do is tell AutoMapper to map from one class to another, as shown next.

Supporting implementation

With the profile written, we'll go back to the controller. Here, we're going to map `CarDto` to the car. Notice the next to last line of this code:

```
        [HttpGet("{id}")]
        public async Task<ActionResult<CarDto>> Get(int id)
        {
```

```
        var car = await _carService.Get(id);
        if (car == null)
        {
            return NotFound();
        }
        var carDto = _mapper.Map<CarDto>(car);

        return carDto;
    }
```

Nothing new or special here, but note that at the bottom of the method, we use a mapper to turn our car into a DTO, which is what we return to the client application.

The only logic in `CarService` is to ensure we have a valid car ID:

```
public async Task<List<CarFlat>> Get(int id)
{
    if (id == 0)
    {
        throw new Exception("Invalid Id");
    }
    return await _carRepository.Get(id);
}
```

This brings us to the repository:

```
public async Task<List<CarFlat?>> Get(int id)
{
    var query = "select * from car c left join options o on o.car_id
    = c.id where c.id = @id";
    using var db = databaseConnectionFactory.GetConnection();
    return (await db.QueryAsync<CarFlat>(query, new {id})).ToList();
}
```

The method is surprisingly simple. We set up and execute the query. Notice that we are using `QueryAsync` and `ToList` as if we were getting all the cars. Actually, what we are getting is a list of the options for a single car, as shown in the next listing:

```
{
    "id": 2,
    "name": "buick skylark 320",
    "mpg": null,
    "cylinders": null,
    "displacement": null,
    "horsepower": null,
```

```
        "weight": null,
        "acceleration": null,
        "modelYear": null,
        "origin": null,
        "is_Deleted": null,
        "options": [
            {
                "optionId": 1,
                "optionName": "Winter Package",
                "optionPrice": 3700
            },
            {

                "optionId": 2,
                "optionName": "Mats",
                "optionPrice": 250
            },
            {

                "optionId": 3,
                "optionName": "Summer Package",
                "optionPrice": 2250
            }
        ]
    }
```

Beautiful! This should look familiar, as it is what we specified at the beginning of the chapter. Each car has its options as a sub-set in the JSON. This will make it much easier to display the cars with their options (e.g., on a web page). Tuck this in your pocket; you don't use it often, but when you need to make this kind of display, the technique is powerful but not obvious.

In this next section, we will introduce Azure Storage Tables, a powerful yet simple way to store data.

Azure Storage Tables

Storage Tables are a great way to persist relatively simple data structures. Creating and using storage tables is quick and easy.

Azure offers a number of ways to store your data. The most popular are SQL Server, Cosmos, and storage tables. Storage tables are the most limited, but they are also the simplest generally speaking, and the fastest to create. They are very popular for keeping track of simple information. For example, you might use storage tables to record each time you send a message or each time something anomalous happens. For these examples, you would enter one row per incident, as described in the following section.

Exploring the essentials

Storage tables are not inherently relational. While you can index, it isn't simple, and it isn't particularly powerful. The reason behind all this is to keep storage tables simple. This makes them ideal for keeping lists, logging, creating progress entries, and so forth.

We will create a storage table that tracks exceptions thrown during the execution of our program. The table we create will look like this on Azure:

☐	ArgumentNullException	TableStorageConsoleAp...	2024-07-23T11:31:15.77...
☐	ArgumentOutOfRangeE...	TableStorageConsoleAp...	2024-07-23T11:31:05.28...
☐	DivideByZeroException	TableStorageConsoleAp...	2024-07-23T11:31:09.47...
☐	IndexOutOfRangeExcept...	TableStorageConsoleAp...	2024-07-23T11:31:11.57...
☐	IndexOutOfRangeExcept...	TableStorageConsoleAp...	2024-07-23T11:31:13.66...
☐	InvalidOperationExcepti...	TableStorageConsoleAp...	2024-07-23T11:31:03.18...
☐	InvalidOperationExcepti...	TableStorageConsoleAp...	2024-07-23T11:31:07.38...

Figure 8.3 – The left portion of a storage table

Due to space concerns, I'm not showing the entire table here. There are columns for the exception type, the time of the exception, the message, and so forth.

To keep things as simple as possible, and to focus 100% on Table Storage, we'll create a console application that simply throws exceptions and stores them in the table. To get started, follow these steps:

1. Create a new project and select **Console App**, as shown in *Figure 8.4*.

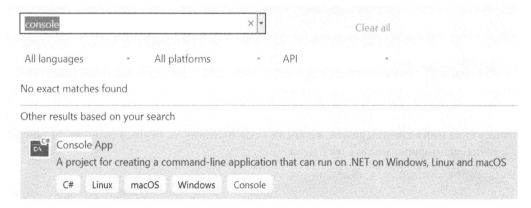

Figure 8.4 – Selecting console app

2. Click **Next** and fill in your project name (I used `TableStorageConsoleApp`), its location on your local disk, and the name of the solution (typically the same as your project). Click **Next** and select **.NET 8** (or later) and, most important, check **Do not use top-level statements**, as shown in the following figure:

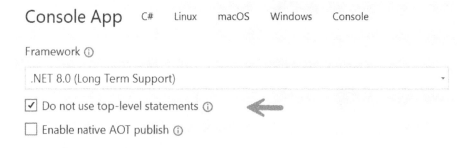

Figure 8.5 – Additional information

3. Click **Create** and your console app will be created, complete with a main entry point and a single line of code, writing the canonical "Hello, World" greeting. You can delete that line.

To keep things simple, we'll have `Main` call `ThrowException`, a method we'll write that will throw a random exception every two seconds. Thus, `Main` is very simple:

```
public class Program
  {
      static void Main(string[] args)
      {
          Console.WriteLine("Loading...");
          for(; ; )
          {
              ThrowException();
          }
      }
  }
```

You can see that `ThrowException` is enclosed in a forever loop and will continue until you close the program. Putting in a more sophisticated way to stop it is, as they say, left as an exercise for the reader.

The job of `ThrowException` is, as said earlier, to throw exceptions randomly. For this, I need nothing more than a `random` generator and a `switch` statement. We begin by enclosing the random generation of exceptions within a try statement:

```
try
{
    Random rand = new Random();
```

```
    var random = rand.Next(0, 10);
    switch (random)
    {
        case 0:
            throw new ArgumentException("Argument Exception");
        case 1:
            throw new ArgumentNullException("Argument Null
            Exception");
        case 2:
            throw new ArgumentOutOfRangeException("Argument Out Of
            Range Exception");
        case 3:
            throw new DivideByZeroException("Divide By Zero
            Exception");
        case 4:
            throw new FileNotFoundException("File Not Found
            Exception");
        case 5:
            throw new FormatException("Format Exception");
        case 6:
            throw new IndexOutOfRangeException("Index Out Of Range
            Exception");
        case 7:
            throw new InvalidOperationException("Invalid Operation
            Exception");
        case 8:
            throw new KeyNotFoundException("Key Not Found Exception");
        case 9:
            throw new NotImplementedException("Not Implemented
            Exception");
        case 10:
            throw new NotSupportedException("Not Supported
            Exception");
        default:
            throw new Exception("Generic Exception - you should never
            see this");
    }
}
```

With that, we can catch each exception and write it to our table:

```
catch (Exception ex)
{
    Console.WriteLine(ex.Message);
```

```
TableModel entity = new TableModel
{
    PartitionKey = ex.GetType().Name,
    RowKey = $"TableStorageConsoleApp-{DateTime.UtcNow.
    ToString("yyyy-MM-ddTHH:mm:ss.fffffffZ")}",
    Message = ex.Message,
    Timestamp = DateTimeOffset.UtcNow
};
TableServiceClient tableServiceClient = new
TableServiceClient("DefaultEndpointsProtocol=
https;AccountName=<your account name>;AccountKey=
<your account key>;EndpointSuffix=core.windows.net");
var storageTableService = new
StorageTableService(tableServiceClient);
storageTableService.UpsertEntityAsync(entity).Wait();
Thread.Sleep(2000);
}
```

There's quite a bit to see here. We begin by creating `TableModel`. We'll create that data structure in just a moment.

Within that model, we'll have `PartitionKey` and `RowKey`. These are critical to `TableStorage`. Together, they make the unique identifier for each row in the table.

All of the entries with the same `PartitionKey` are clustered, and in that cluster are all their `RowKeys`. This makes retrieval infinitely faster. Rather than having to scan through all the `RowKeys`, retrieval can be achieved by jumping to the right `PartitionKey` and searching from there.

We also store the exception's message and the current time as a timestamp.

`TableServiceClient` is supplied by the NuGet package (see requirements at the beginning of this chapter). The address you'll initialize with is supplied by Azure as shown later in this chapter.

We then call `UpsertEntityAsync`, passing in the entity we created earlier, and go to sleep for two seconds (the amount of time you sleep is entirely up to you).

Please note that you will need your own `AccountKey` and preferably your own `accountName`.

TableModel

I promised earlier to show you the `TableModel`. It is quite simple, just enough to capture the essential information:

```
public class TableModel : ITableEntity
{
    required public string PartitionKey { get; set; }
```

```
    required public string RowKey { get; set; }
    public DateTimeOffset? Timestamp { get; set; }
    public string? Message { get; set; }
    public ETag ETag { get; set; } = ETag.All;
}
```

Note that ETag must be in every table model. This is used for optimistic concurrency during updates. We won't be doing updates and don't care about this except that it must be there.

StorageTableService

The heart of the application is StorageTableService. Here is where UpsertEntityAsync lives, which does the work of interacting with our table:

```
public async Task<Response> UpsertEntityAsync(TableModel entity)
{
    var response = await _tableCreationTask;
    var table = _tableServiceClient.GetTableClient(response.Value.
    Name);
    return await table.UpsertEntityAsync(entity);
}
```

To get started, we declare two member variables at the top of the class:

```
private readonly TableServiceClient _tableServiceClient;
private readonly Task<Response<TableItem>> _tableCreationTask;
```

Notice that the second member is of type Task<Response<TableItem>. Both Response and TableItem are supplied by the Azure NuGet package. The constructor takes TableServiceClient (also supplied in the same NuGet package).

```
public StorageTableService(TableServiceClient tableServiceClient)
{
    _tableServiceClient = tableServiceClient;
    _tableCreationTask = _tableServiceClient.
    CreateTableIfNotExistsAsync("ExceptionsTable");
}
```

It is here that we create the table if it doesn't exist and name it ExceptionsTable (feel free to name yours whatever you like).

All the Upsert method needs to do is call tableCreationTask and wait to get back Response<TableItem>. With that in hand, it is ready to call GetTableClient on TableServiceClient, passing in the name of the table. Finally, we call UpsertEntityAsync on the table passing in TableModel.

Please make sure you understand the previous paragraph as it is the heart of working with `StorageTables`.

Populating the table in Azure

With what we've written, populating the table in Azure is automatic. Run the program; your output should look something like *Figure 8.6*.

```
Loading ...
File Not Found Exception
Invalid Operation Exception
Specified argument was out of the range of valid values. (Parameter 'Argument Out Of Range Exception')
Divide By Zero Exception
File Not Found Exception
Index Out Of Range Exception
Value cannot be null. (Parameter 'Argument Null Exception')
Index Out Of Range Exception
Divide By Zero Exception
Not Implemented Exception
Value cannot be null. (Parameter 'Argument Null Exception')
Specified argument was out of the range of valid values. (Parameter 'Argument Out Of Range Exception')
```

Figure 8.6 – Generated exceptions

> **Note**
>
> You'll need an Azure account for this part. As noted earlier, you can get a free starter account at the link provided.

Now, let's go to Azure and see what we've got:

1. Log in to your account and click on **Home** and then on **Storage browser**, as shown in the following figure:

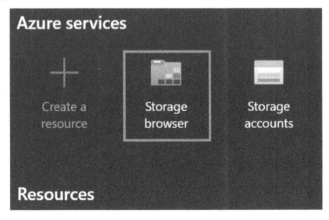

Figure 8.7 – Storage browser

2. From there, click on your `TableStorage` account. That will bring up a dashboard. Click on **Tables**, as shown in *Figure 8.8*.

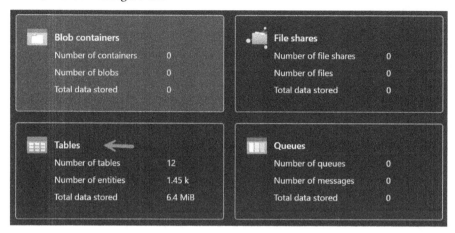

Figure 8.8 – Selecting tables

3. You should be brought to a page where your tables should be listed as links. Click on the table we created. The entries that match what we saw in the application will pop up, as shown (in part) in *Figure 8.9*.

PartitionKey	RowKey	Timestamp	Message
ArgumentNullException	TableStorageConsoleAp...	2024-07-23T18:21:20.09...	Value cannot be null. (Pa...
ArgumentNullException	TableStorageConsoleAp...	2024-07-23T18:21:28.56...	Value cannot be null. (Pa...
ArgumentOutOfRangeE...	TableStorageConsoleAp...	2024-07-23T18:21:11.65...	Specified argument was ...
ArgumentOutOfRangeE...	TableStorageConsoleAp...	2024-07-23T18:21:30.66...	Specified argument was ...
DivideByZeroException	TableStorageConsoleAp...	2024-07-23T18:21:13.80...	Divide By Zero Exception
DivideByZeroException	TableStorageConsoleAp...	2024-07-23T18:21:24.32...	Divide By Zero Exception
FileNotFoundException	TableStorageConsoleAp...	2024-07-23T18:21:07.42...	File Not Found Exception
FileNotFoundException	TableStorageConsoleAp...	2024-07-23T18:21:15.90...	File Not Found Exception
FileNotFoundException	TableStorageConsoleAp...	2024-07-23T18:21:39.06...	File Not Found Exception

Figure 8.9 – The table on Azure

Notice that the entries are not in the order in which they were created. Rather, they are clustered by `PartitionKey`, as described earlier.

Shockingly, that's all there is to it.

Introducing Microsoft Aspire

Microsoft has introduced Aspire, which it describes as *opinionated, cloud ready stack for building observable, Production-ready, distributed applications*. Say what?

In this case, *opinionated* means that there are conventions and templates to make life easier. With this and all things, you can customize, but the more you follow the conventions, the easier it is to write, and perhaps more important, to read your code.

Cloud-ready stack indicates that you will be working locally but on code that can easily be moved to the cloud (read Azure). *Production-ready* indicates that what you build will be non-trivial and ready to roll out, and *distributed* means that you will be creating micro-services hosted in containers, in our case, Docker.

Aspire provides you with a number of services that you could write yourself, but no longer have to. Instead, you get fully tested code *automagically* that provides, among other things, storage, messaging, and web services, and that can also provide interoperability with databases, caching, and more.

> **Note**
> You can use Aspire with Visual Studio Code or even the .NET CLI, but we'll stick with Visual Studio.

Sample program

Aspire is very powerful, but it can be tricky to get all the pieces in place. We *could* write our own sample program, but that would be silly since Microsoft supplies one that you can create with just a few keystrokes in Visual Studio. To get started, follow these steps:

1. Create a new project and select **.NET Aspire Starter Application**. Be sure to choose the one for C#, as shown in *Figure 8.10*:

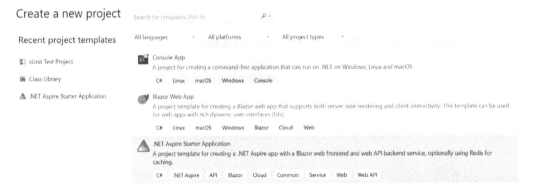

Figure 8.10 - Choosing Aspire

2. Enter a project name (I'll use `AspirePackt`) and leave the rest of the values as their defaults.

3. On the next page, make sure you select **.NET 8** and **Use Redis for caching**, and while you always should create unit tests, we'll skip that for now (in a "real" application, you want those unit tests), as shown in *Figure 8.11*:

Additional information

.NET Aspire Starter Application   C#   .NET Aspire   API   Blazor   Cloud

Framework ⓘ

.NET 8.0 (Long Term Support)	▾

☑ Configure for HTTPS ⓘ

☑ Use Redis for caching (requires a supported container runtime) ⓘ

☐ Create a tests project ⓘ

Figure 8.11 – Selecting the frameworks

Here's what we're going to see: a sample weather app that supports caching. It will get the weather through an API, using random, demonstration values.

1. Start the app up and the first thing that will happen is that the .NET Aspire dashboard will open in your browser, as partly shown in *Figure 8.12*.

Type	Name	State	Source	Endpoints
Container	cache	● Running	docker.io/library/redis:7.2	tcp://localhost:60474
Project	apiservice	● Running	AspirePackt.ApiService.csproj	+2
Project	webfrontend	● Running	AspirePackt.Web.csproj	https://localhost:7225, +1

Figure 8.12 – Aspire dashboard

This was all created for you in the sample program, which also created a Blazor application that will be used to display the data retrieved by the API.

Notice that the third line's project in *Figure 8.13* is webfrontend. Click on the URL and you are brought to the iconic **Hello, world!** page. On the left are three buttons, as shown in the following figure:

Figure 8.13 – The running application

Now click on the **Weather** option and *voilà*! The API is hit, and the weather data is displayed, as shown in *Figure 8.14*.

Weather

This component demonstrates showing data loaded from a backend API service.

Date	Temp. (C)	Temp. (F)	Summary
6/9/2024	-14	7	Mild
6/10/2024	-19	-2	Cool
6/11/2024	-8	18	Mild
6/12/2024	4	39	Balmy
6/13/2024	35	94	Hot

Figure 8.14 – The displayed weather from the API

If you refresh the screen a few times, you'll see that it is instantly responsive as it is using the cache. After about 10 seconds, it will generate new data.

Exploring the Aspire dashboard

Going back to *Figure 8.12*, we see a number of useful features. Click on **Resources**, for example, to see a list of information for all the .NET projects in your application. These include the app state, endpoints, and environment variables.

Console displays (surprise!) the console output from each project.

The **Structured** option displays logs as tables. You can filter and search (either free-form or filtered). You can expand the details for each entry by clicking on the **View** button on the far right.

The **Traces** button displays the request paths throughout your application. Locate a request for **Weather** and select **View**. The dashboard will display the request in stages.

Click on **ApiService | View** and you'll see the time it took to hit the API. Click on **View** on the right and the resources are displayed in detail. Scroll down to see more details.

Finally, the **Metrics** button will display instruments and meters, as they are available for your application.

What have you learned, Dorothy?

As you can see, the sample application consists of a number of projects. The first, perhaps most essential is the app host, which acts as the orchestrator. It will automatically set `IsAspireHost` in the project file to true.

Pour through the `Program.cs` file and you'll see what you'd expect as an API developer, along with Aspire in `APIService` (and a couple of things added for Blazor).

Note that the first line creates `DistributedApplication` using Docker.

A critical line in this file is `AspirePackt.ApiService`, which configures the service discovery and communication among the projects in your solution. The name (`apiservice`) identifies the project and is used by projects that want to communicate with it.

Another important and universal project is `ServiceDefaults`, which is a shared project that manages configurations so that they can be used across projects. This allows the application to have all the services share service discovery, telemetry, and more.

Adding Aspire to an existing app

We all love green-field projects, but the reality is that most of the time we're working with existing code. Aspire would not be very interesting if it only worked from scratch, but fortunately, you can add Aspire to existing applications.

We could add Aspire to our car application, but once again, Microsoft assists, providing a reasonably complex application for us to work with. To get started, clone their application by using the following command:

```
git clone https://github.com/MicrosoftDocs/mslearn-dotnet-cloudnative-
devops.git eShopLite
```

This sample consists of three projects:

- Data Entities is a class library that defines the `Product` class
- `Products` is a web API that returns a list of all the Products in the store's catalog
- `Store` is a Blazor web app that displays the products on a website

Note that we will not be focusing on Blazor. We will use it only as far as it is part of this example

Getting oriented with our new project

Let's take a look at what the new project (out of the box) looks like. To do so, follow these steps to create our "existing" project that we will add Aspire to:

1. Open `eShopLite.sln`. Right-click on the solution and select **Configure Startup Projects**.

2. Choose multiple startup projects and in the **Action** column, select **Start** for **Products and Store**, as shown in the following figure:

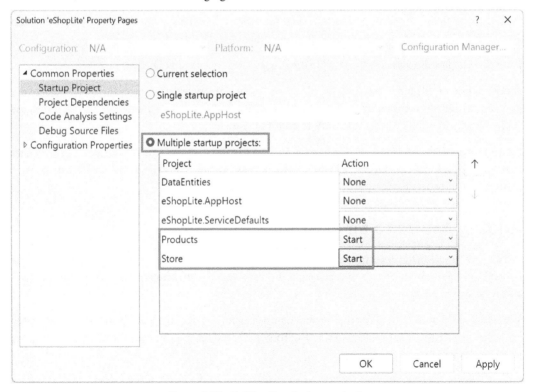

Figure 8.15 – Setting the startup projects

3.   Fire it up by pressing *F5* and note that two browser pages open. One page has the raw JSON and the second page is a simple browser application that lets you view that data (click on **Products**), as shown in part in *Figure 8.15*.

Figure 8.16 – The raw JSON

At the top of the JSON is a checkbox for pretty print. That will take this raw JSON and make it more readable, as shown in the following figure:

Figure 8.17 – Pretty print

Blazor will give you a web-based view of that same data, as shown in *Figure 8.18*:

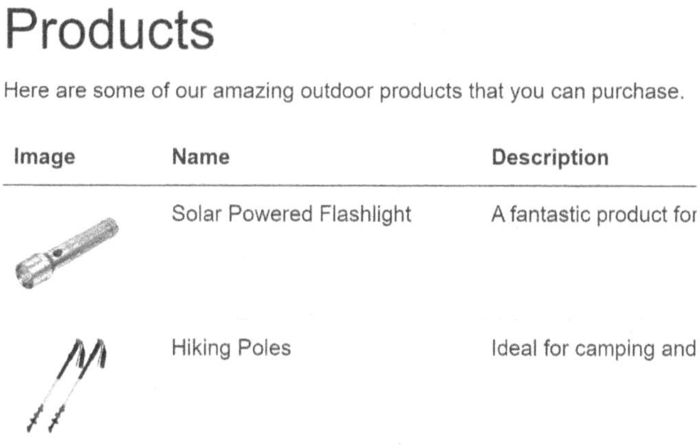

Products

Here are some of our amazing outdoor products that you can purchase.

Image	Name	Description
	Solar Powered Flashlight	A fantastic product for
	Hiking Poles	Ideal for camping and

Figure 8.18 – The browser display of the products

Now that we have a working application, let's refactor it to add Aspire. We'll do that next.

Adding Aspire

Now that we have a working API solution, let's add Aspire. To do so, follow these steps:

1. Right-click on one of the projects (I'll use **Store**) and select **Add | .Net Aspire Orchestrator Support**. That brings up the dialog box.

2. Click **OK** and two new projects are added to your solution:

    *   eShopLiteAppHost

    *   eShopLite.ServiceDefaults

Spend a few minutes exploring these projects. The first, eShopLiteAppHost, is an orchestrator project whose job is to connect (and configure) the various projects and services of your application. It is automatically set as the startup project. eShopServiceDefaults holds configurations that will be used across projects, especially service discovery and telemetry (more about these shortly).

1. Next, open Program.cs in AppHost, where you will see this code:

    ```
    builder.AddProject<Projects.Store>("store");
    ```

    This registers the store project in the orchestrator. We now need to register the Products project.

2. Right-click on it and select **Add | .NET Aspire Orchestrator Support**. You'll get a dialog saying the orchestrator already exists; just click **OK**.

3. Go back to AppHost/Program.cs and you can see that another line has been added, as you might expect:

    ```
    builder.AddProject<Projects.Products>("Products");
    ```

Now comes the fun part. Store needs to be able to find Products' backend address. Rather than doing this by hand, we turn that responsibility over to the orchestrator.

Discovery

While both projects are registered with the orchestrator, Store needs to be able to discover the Products' backend address. To enable discovery, return to Program.cs and add a reference to the Products project. Your program.cs file should now look like this:

```
var builder = DistributedApplication.CreateBuilder(args);

var Products = builder.AddProject<Projects.Products>("Products");

builder.AddProject<Projects.Store>("store")
```

```
        .WithExternalHttpEndpoints()
        .WithReference(Products);

builder.Build().Run();
```

> **Note**
>
> If you want to deploy this application, you'll need to call `WithExternalHttpEndpoints` to make sure it is public to the outside world.

Almost done. We need to update `appsettings.json` in the `Store` project:

```json
{
  "DetailedErrors": true,
  "Logging": {
    "LogLevel": {
      "Default": "Information",
      "Microsoft.AspNetCore": "Warning"
    }
  },
  "AllowedHosts": "*",
  "ProductEndpoint": "http://Products",
  "ProductEndpointHttps": "https://Products"
}
```

The addresses for both endpoints now use the `Products` name. Note that these names are used to discover the address of the `Products` project.

Press *F5* to run it. You've added Aspire, with all its features and dashboard, to your existing API project.

Summary

In this chapter, you learned about three very powerful, advanced techniques. First, we looked at creating more complex APIs that return hierarchical data. We did this by adding and presenting options for each car type.

Next, we looked at Azure Storage Tables, a lightweight way to store data on Azure, side-stepping the complexity of Entity Framework and Cosmos.

Finally, we went on to look at Microsoft's Aspire dashboard, a very powerful and useful tool for working with APIs.

In the next chapter, we'll look at the critical issue of authentication and authorization, without which you cannot create an enterprise API.

You try it

Creating an Aspire dashboard is pretty straightforward out of the box, but creating hierarchical data is not. To take on a challenge, create a program that displays a few states and with them their principal cities. The result might look something like this:

```
{
    "statePostalCode": MA,
    "name": "Massachusetts",
    "capital": Boston,
    "cities": [
        {
            "city" : "Worchester",
            "longitude": "100.01.93",
            "latitude": -907-45-33
        },
        {
            "city": Acton,
            "longitude": "100.01.107",
            "latitude": -10-398-405
        },
    ]
}
```

Feel free to make up the longitude and latitude, or look it up online. You'll want at least two to three cities and two to three states. Once you have your structure, save it as a flat file in an Azure Storage Table.

9

Authentication
and Authorization

In the previous chapter, we reviewed a number of advanced API topics. In this chapter, you will learn how to add authentication (which answers questions such as "is this user who they say they are?") and authorization ("is this user allowed to take this action?"). We will use the Azure function from *Chapter 6*.

In this chapter, we will cover the following topics:

- Differences between authentication and authorization
- Definitions of authentication and authorization
- A walkthrough of authentication – proving who you are
- A walkthrough of authorization – testing if you can take a specific action

Technical requirements

For this chapter, you will need the following:

1. Visual Studio
2. An Azure Account (you can get a free starter account at `https://azure.mcrosoft.com`)

Note that much of this chapter relies on the code and action from *Chapter 6*. If you don't have the code, you can download it from the repository: `https://github.com/PacktPublishing/Programming-APIs-with-C-Sharp-and-.NET/tree/main/Chapter06`

The code for this chapter is available at `https://github.com/PacktPublishing/Programming-APIs-with-C-Sharp-and-.NET/tree/main/Chapter09`

Introduction to authentication and authorization

The vast majority of applications will need some form of **authentication and authorization** (**A&A**). Authentication is the process of proving who you are, while authorization is the process of determining whether you have permission to do what you are trying to do. Typically, you authenticate first, perhaps once per session, and then authorization is checked for each action you attempt.

There are many different types of A&A, but since we're focusing mostly on Azure, we'll use their built-in feature set colloquially known as **Easy Auth**.

Overview of A&A

Though there are many kinds of A&A, including many nuances such as the authentication of services, users, and so on, we'll focus on A&A for a single user in an Azure Tenant. That will usually be an employee during debugging (you!). This will then allow you to extend these concepts so that other services you create can be authorized in the same way.

> Tenant
>
> A tenant in Azure is a Guid that specifies all the content of a single organization.

Enabling authentication on existing functions

Let's begin by adding authentication to an existing Azure function. To do so, follow these steps:

1. Open your Azure Function resource from *Chapter 6* and navigate to the **Authentication** section, as shown in *Figure 9.1*.

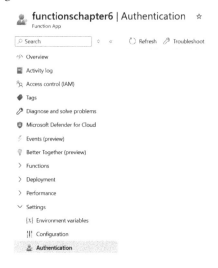

Figure 9.1 – Selecting Authentication

2. Click **Add Identity Provider**, and then select **Microsoft**. Use the following configuration options (they are almost all default):

- **Choose a tenant**

  - **Workforce configuration** (default)

- **App registration**

  - **App registration type**: **Create new app registration** (default)

  - **Name**: The default is likely the name of your existing Function App resource; in this case, it is **Functions**.

  - **Client secret expiration**: **Recommended: 180 days** (default)

  - **Supported account types**: **Current tenant – Single tenant** (default)

- **Additional checks** (default)

  - **Client application requirement**: **Allow requests only from this application itself** (default)

  - **Identity requirement**: **Allow requests from any identity** (default)

  - **Tenant requirement**: **Allow requests only from the issuer tenant** (your tenant GUID goes here)

- **App Service authentication settings** (default)

  - **Restrict access**: **Require authentication** (default)

  - **Unauthenticated requests**: **HTTP 401 Unauthorized: recommended for APIs** (default)

- **Token Store: Checked**

To put this all together, see *Figure 9.2*.

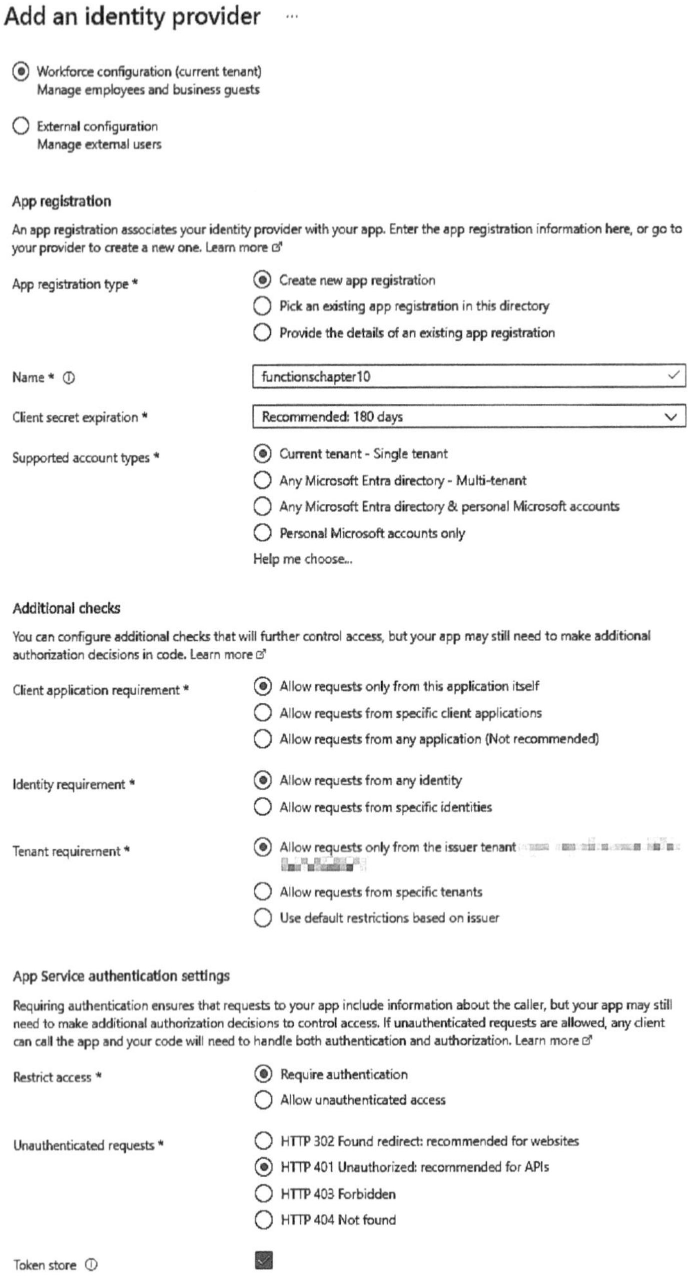

Add an identity provider   ...

⦿ Workforce configuration (current tenant)
  Manage employees and business guests

◯ External configuration
  Manage external users

App registration

An app registration associates your identity provider with your app. Enter the app registration information here, or go to your provider to create a new one. Learn more ☑

App registration type *   ⦿ Create new app registration
                                   ◯ Pick an existing app registration in this directory
                                   ◯ Provide the details of an existing app registration

Name * ⓘ | functionschapter10   ✓ |

Client secret expiration * | Recommended: 180 days   ∨ |

Supported account types *   ⦿ Current tenant - Single tenant
                                   ◯ Any Microsoft Entra directory - Multi-tenant
                                   ◯ Any Microsoft Entra directory & personal Microsoft accounts
                                   ◯ Personal Microsoft accounts only
                                   Help me choose...

Additional checks

You can configure additional checks that will further control access, but your app may still need to make additional authorization decisions in code. Learn more ☑

Client application requirement *   ⦿ Allow requests only from this application itself
                                   ◯ Allow requests from specific client applications
                                   ◯ Allow requests from any application (Not recommended)

Identity requirement *   ⦿ Allow requests from any identity
                                   ◯ Allow requests from specific identities

Tenant requirement *   ⦿ Allow requests only from the issuer tenant ▨▨▨ ▨▨ ▨▨▨▨▨ ▨▨▨
                                     ▨▨▨▨▨▨▨
                                   ◯ Allow requests from specific tenants
                                   ◯ Use default restrictions based on issuer

App Service authentication settings

Requiring authentication ensures that requests to your app include information about the caller, but your app may still need to make additional authorization decisions to control access. If unauthenticated requests are allowed, any client can call the app and your code will need to handle both authentication and authorization. Learn more ☑

Restrict access *   ⦿ Require authentication
                                   ◯ Allow unauthenticated access

Unauthenticated requests *   ◯ HTTP 302 Found redirect: recommended for websites
                                   ⦿ HTTP 401 Unauthorized: recommended for APIs
                                   ◯ HTTP 403 Forbidden
                                   ◯ HTTP 404 Not found

Token store ⓘ   ☑

Figure 9.2 – Adding an identity provider

3. We can skip **Permissions** for now, so click **Add**.

You will be returned to your **Authentication** blade, showing your new Microsoft Identity provider.

4. Click on the name of your Identity provider or navigate back to the main Azure portal. Click on **Microsoft Entra ID**, select **App registrations**, then your app.

This is your configuration area to manage various things about the app's authentication. We'll be editing this in a bit but try to run or navigate to your existing Function app's HTTP trigger like you did in *Chapter 6*. You should see that it now shows **401 error (Unauthorized)**.

Next, we'll authenticate to the new Identity Provider in two ways to give you an idea of different use cases.

Programmatically accessing your API

Open your Function in Visual Studio from *Chapter 6*. Right-click on the solution in **Solution Explorer** and click on **Add New Project... Add a .NET Console app**. Add the Azure.Identity NuGet package, and then create a DefaultAzureCredential instance.

There are many different credential classes that inherit from a TokenCredential base class implementing different use cases, but the DefaultAzureCredential tries a number of different credentials in order so that it can easily be used in several different scenarios. Use the following boilerplate code to securely call your Function:

```
DefaultAzureCredential cred = new DefaultAzureCredential(new
DefaultAzureCredentialOptions
        {
            TenantId = <your tenant ID>
        });
Azure.Core.AccessToken token = await cred.GetTokenAsync(new Azure.
Core.TokenRequestContext(new string[]
        {
            <clientId>
        }), CancellationToken.None);
var message = new HttpRequestMessage(HttpMethod.Get, "https://<your
function resource>.azurewebsites.net/api/Function1");
        message.Headers.Authorization = new
        AuthenticationHeaderValue("Bearer", token.Token);
        HttpResponseMessage resp = await new HttpClient().
        SendAsync(message);//inject the HttpClient in a production
                            //app
        resp.EnsureSuccessStatusCode();
        string content = await resp.Content.ReadAsStringAsync();
        Console.WriteLine(content);
```

Try to run it now, and it should throw an error on `resp.EnsureSuccessStatusCode();`. This is because we have not told our API that you as a user (via Visual Studio's helper authentication client) are allowed to make calls to your API.

In a development environment, we can authorize the well-known client ID to the API. To do so, in the Azure Portal, navigate to your Function resource again:

1. In the **Authentication** blade, click the pencil icon under the **Edit** heading.
2. Select **Allow Requests From Specific Client Applications** if it isn't already selected, and then add **04f0c124-f2bc-4f59-8241-bf6df9866bbd**. Click **OK** and then **Save**.

    We'll be doing this again later in this chapter.

3. Go back to Visual Studio and run the console application again.

The call to your API should now succeed and will print out the data you configured in your API's Environment variables blade in *Chapter 6*.

Next, we'll try to use `ClientSecretCredential`. To do so, follow these instructions:

1. Navigate to the **Certificates & Secrets** blade in the app registration and click **New Client Secret**.
2. Enter a description and expiration time, and click **Add**.
3. Copy the value somewhere (e.g., Notepad), as you will not be able to access it again. Modify the code by adding a new `ClientSecretCredential` instance instead of the existing credentials you might already have. You'll need the Tenant ID and Client ID available in the **Overview** blade:

    ```
    ClientSecretCredential cred = new
    ClientSecretCredential(<tenantId>, <clientId>, <clientSecret>);
    ```

The existing call to `GetTokenAsync` should work without changes. The rest of the code including the HTTP call itself should run successfully as is, and you should again see your configured API string.

> **Note**
> All of the preceding strings are available in the code from *Chapter 6*.

Authorizing additional Azure Resources

You'll almost certainly need additional Azure services to complement your cloud solution, so let's try to authorize one to call your API. To do so, follow these instructions:

1. Go to the Azure portal, and then your existing Resource group. Create a new Logic app, and select **Consumption** for hosting.
2. Give it a name and select the same **Region** that your other Resources are in.

3. When it completes deployment, select the **Identity blade**, change the **Status** to **On**, and click **Save** and then **Yes**.

4. Select the Logic app designer blade. Add a new HTTP trigger, enter your deployed Function URI (likely `https://<my resource name>.azurewebsites.net/api/Function1`), and the `GET` method.

5. Click **Show All** for **Advanced parameters** and select **Managed Identity** under **Authentication Type**. It should resemble *Figure 9.3*.

Figure 9.3 – Advanced Parameters

6. Click **Save**. Go back to the **Overview** blade and click **Run**.

7. Click on the **Trigger history** tab and notice that it is red, indicating a failure.

8. Click on the failed trigger, and then click the **Outputs** link. It should show **403 error (Forbidden)**, indicating that the service authenticated you correctly, but you were not authorized.

    To authorize this Logic app to call your Function API, we need to add its client ID to the list of authorized clients that can call your API.

9. Go back to **Azure Portal Home** and click on **Microsoft Entra ID**. Search for your Logic app's name in the **Search Your Tenant** text box. It should have an entry under the **Enterprise Applications** section.

10. Next, click on that and then copy the GUID under **Application ID**.

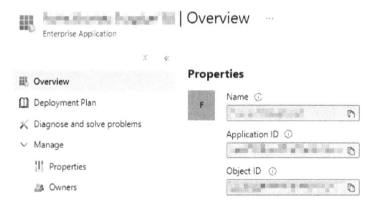

Figure 9.4 – Authorization

Note

Some of the fields in *Figure 9.4* have been obscured as a security measure.

---

11. Navigate back to your Function app. Find the **Authentication** blade, and then click on the pencil as we did before. Next, click the other pencil icon next to **Allowed client applications**, and add a new entry with the GUID you just copied, as shown in *Figure 9.5*.

Figure 9.5 – Adding allowed client applications

12. Click **OK** and then **Save**.

13. Navigate back to the Logic app, and then click on **Run | Run**. This should immediately start another run of your Logic app calling your API.

14. Click on the **Trigger history** tab on the **Overview** blade. You should see that the latest one has a green status, indicating success, as shown in *Figure 9.6*.

Figure 9.6 – Success!

If the start time does not match up to what you are expecting, you may have to click **Refresh** at the top of the blade. Click the green success indicator and click on **Outputs** again. The statusCode should now be **200 (OK)**, and you should once again see the text you configured in the **Function Environment** variables blade.

Summary

In this chapter, you learned the difference between A&A. You then saw how to use the Azure controls to establish authentication and authorization for a specific Azure resource. In the next chapter, we will learn about **Continuous Integration and Continuous Deployment (CI/CD)** on Azure.

You try it

Using the deployed function from *Chapter 6*, authenticate yourself and give yourself authorization. Ensure this succeeds by creating a console app. Then create a Logic app and then authorize it to call your API.

10

Deploying to Azure

In this chapter, we will explore **Continuous Integration and Continuous Deployment (CI/CD)** on Azure. These are critical skills for enterprise development and ensure that bugs are caught early in the process, especially when working with a team. The earlier integration issues are surfaced, the less expensive they are to fix.

Among the skills that we will review are creating an Azure project, creating a pipeline, and configuring the pipeline for CI/CD.

This chapter will build on the skills you developed in *Chapter 6* and walk you through setting up CI/CD step by step.

We will cover the following topics in this chapter:

- Using tests to ensure code quality
- Deploying from DevOps
- Deploying to Azure

Technical requirements

For this chapter, you'll need the following:

- Visual Studio
- The `Azure.Data.Tables` NuGet package

Getting started

At the end of *Chapter 6*, you saw how easy it is to deploy to Azure directly from Visual Studio. This is fine for testing scenarios and one-off experiments or proofs of concept, but in a production scenario, this one project may be part of a much larger system.

Setting up a series of "gates" (checks) before publishing to production can be advantageous for many reasons. Note that there are many types of release gates. The most common (and important) are **Pull Requests (PRs)**, unit tests, integration tests, and end-to-end tests.

Using tests to ensure code quality

There are many kinds of tests that you might run against your code. Among the most important are the following:

- Unit tests
- Integration tests
- Automated tests

Unit tests cover one section of your code that does one thing. For example, many unit tests have a 1:1 correspondence with methods, but not always. Think functionality rather than code. However, they must run extremely fast so that you run them after every code change. This allows you to code with confidence, knowing that if anything breaks, you know that something went wrong and where the problem is located.

Integration tests are run less often, typically after completing a discreet set of functionality to make sure that what you've created fits together with what is already in place. Finally, end-to-end tests ensure that the entire set of scenarios works as expected. This is, typically, where professional QA people run their tests. As programmers, it is almost impossible to run thorough end-to-end tests on our own code: we see what we expect to see, and we run what we expect the user to run. QA professionals can create a suite of tests to ensure that the program works well with good data but also with bad or corrupted data and when the user does something we didn't expect.

Fortunately, you can automate all of these tests, checking various levels of the code to ensure nothing has regressed. While we won't be looking at all of the advanced scenarios that Azure DevOps provides for us, we will be setting up a standard build and release pipeline that you can use to automate your deployments. In short, we will set up CI that will automate what we just did when we manually published to Azure.

Manual versus automated implementation

Going a little deeper, let's compare DevOps (continuous delivery) and publishing through Visual Studio manually. You can have automated builds whenever a new commit has been pushed to master. Along with automated builds on a branch, you can have builds checked with PRs. PRs have the benefit of another skilled programmer checking and testing your code before it is merged in. The fact is that automated tests can only go so far. PRs are also a good place to determine and test which environments your code requires (e.g., Windows, Linux, etc.).

Using the same binaries

It is highly advantageous to deploy exactly the same binaries to your lower environments, such as your local computer, and then promote these same binaries to production. Though C# and .NET do have deterministic builds, the other parts of your deployed package or container may not. If something does go wrong after deployment, DevOps provides the ability to immediately roll back your deployed artifact. A history of these deployments is kept for each environment as well.

While DevOps is superior in a lot of scenarios, it can be somewhat more difficult when debugging build failures. Each step of the build pipeline is logged for you to look at and diagnose later; however, that is sometimes easier said than done. Additionally, the more concurrent pipeline builds there are, the more difficult it may be to figure out what went wrong in the case of a failure. Compounding this, the larger the team gets, the more queueing of builds may happen.

With that in place, we are ready to deploy to DevOps.

> **Tip**
> The number of concurrent executing pipelines and the execution minutes per month is limited in the free version of DevOps. You can, of course, subscribe to increase these restrictions.

Deploying from DevOps

We'll now be walking through deploying from DevOps instead of our local Visual Studio. The first step is to create your DevOps project, as shown in *Figure 10.1*:

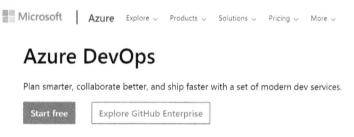

Figure 10.1 – DevOps opening page

To create the project, we'll use the wizard. (The first time, the wizard will probably come up immediately, otherwise click to bring up the wizard.) Here are the steps:

1. Go to dev.Azure.com.

2. Click on **Start free** (even if you already have an account).

3. If it redirects you, enter dev.azure.com in the address box.

4. Click **New Project** in the upper right.

5. Enter a name and description and choose **private**.

6. Click on **Advanced** and make sure the version control is set to **Git**.

7. Click **Create**.

Let's now import a bit of code.

Importing sample code

Before we can deploy to Azure, we need to have a repository with the code we want to deploy. Clone the code for *Chapter 6* from `https://github.com/PacktPublishing/Programming-APIs-with-C-Sharp-and-.NET/tree/main/Chapter06` and copy or move it into another folder so that it is no longer associated with the cloned repo. Open the solution in Visual Studio. Now we want to use Visual Studio to create a repository in our new DevOps project. Here are the steps:

1. Open the **GitChanges** view.

2. Click **Create Git Repository**.

3. Select **Azure DevOps**, as shown in *Figure 10.2*, and click on **Create and Push**.

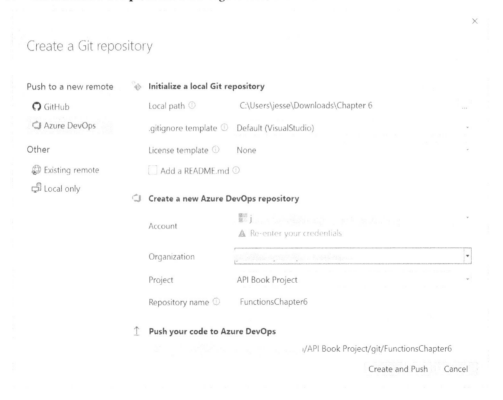

Figure 10.2 – Create a Git repository

With that in place, we are ready to create the actual build pipeline.

Creating the build pipeline

Now that you have your code in an Azure repository, you can create the build pipeline. To do so, take the following steps:

1. Click on **Create Pipeline**, as shown in *Figure 10.3*:

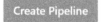

Figure 10.3 – Create Pipeline

You should see a wizard that will walk you through creating your pipeline.

The first step asks where your code is. DevOps supports a few different code repositories, including Azure Repos, Bitbucket, GitHub, GitHub Enterprise, other generic Git repositories, and Subversion.

> **Note**
> There are two different ways to build your pipelines. The first is through YAML files, which can be in your repository alongside your code, which has the added benefit of being versioned. The second supported way to build your pipelines is the way we'll be taking.

2. Click on **Use the classic editor**, which will give us a much more in-depth UI to create a pipeline without YAML

3. Choose your repository in the next dropdown and then select the default branch, as shown in *Figure 10.4*:

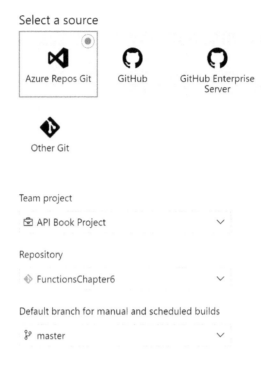

Figure 10.4 – Select a source

4. Click **Continue** and you will see a screen that asks you to select a template for your project. A number of standard ones are displayed by default but there are many others available. Since we are building and deploying an Azure function, scroll down to where it lists **Azure Functions for .NET**, as shown in *Figure 10.5*, and click **Apply**.

Figure 10.5 – Azure Functions for .NET

This takes you to an editor for your pipeline. You should see various tabs, including **Tasks**, **Variable**, **Triggers**, **Options**, and **History**.

5. The pipeline item under the **Tasks** tab should be selected by default. If not, select it. In either case, click it and then rename your pipeline to whatever you would like.

The agent pool allows you to select from Microsoft-hosted build machines or, if you have custom private agents set up, you can also select those. We will not be covering private agents in this book.

6. Select **Azure Pipelines** for the agent pool, and select **ubuntu latest** for **Agent Specification**, as shown in *Figure 10.6*.

> **Note**
> Although leaving the agent specification as Windows may work, we find it prevents a number of issues when you match your agent specification to the resource type that you created in Azure. In our case, we made a Linux Azure function.

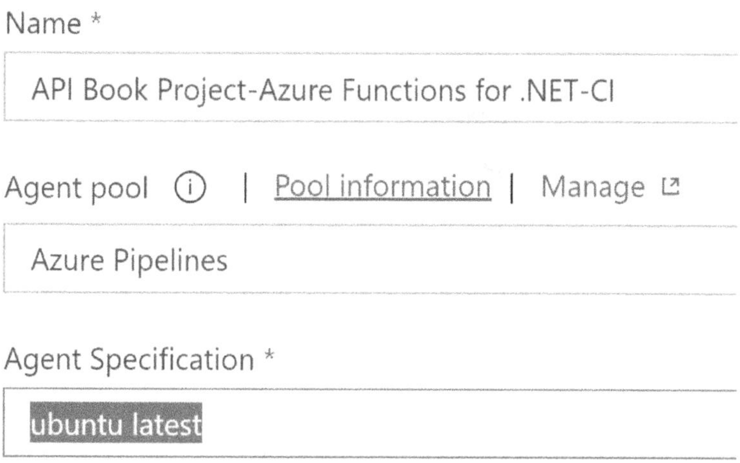

Name *

API Book Project-Azure Functions for .NET-CI

Agent pool ⓘ | Pool information | Manage ↗

Azure Pipelines

Agent Specification *

ubuntu latest

Figure 10.6 – Pipeline setup

7. Select **Get Sources** under the **Tasks** tab. This should already be filled out for you with a number of defaults, including your default branch to build from. The defaults for **Agent job 1** under the **Get sources** item should be fine and can be retained as is. Click on **Build Project** under **Agent job 1** to select the actual task that is used to build the published output, as shown in *Figure 10.7*.

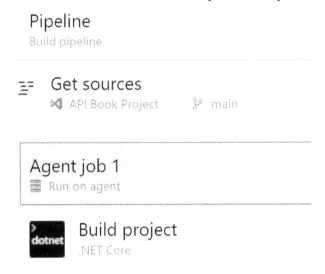

Figure 10.7 – Get sources

The default task should be **Build Project .NET Core**. You can build a number of different types of assemblies, including console, libraries, ASP.NET Core, and, in our case, Azure Functions. As of the time of writing, task version 2 is currently supported and is the default.

8. Change the display name to something more descriptive, such as Publish Project.

9. Select **publish** from the **Command** dropdown. Uncheck **Publish web projects**. Though our Azure function is an API and could be considered a web project in a different context, we do not need this particular functionality for what we are doing. Leave the arguments as is.

10. Ensure that **Zip published projects** and **Add project's folder name to publish path** are both checked.

11. In the **Arguments** text box, change `publish_output` to `$(build.artifactstagingdirectory)`, as shown in *Figure 10.8*.

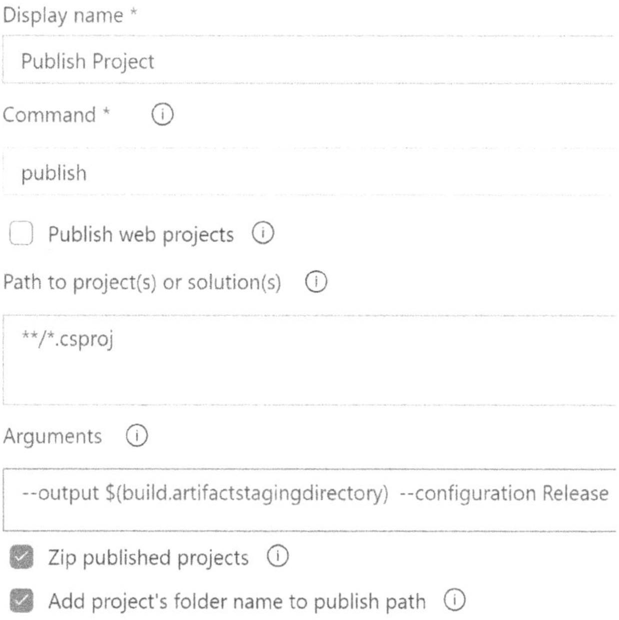

Display name *

Publish Project

Command *   ⓘ

publish

☐ Publish web projects ⓘ

Path to project(s) or solution(s) ⓘ

**/*.csproj

Arguments ⓘ

--output $(build.artifactstagingdirectory) --configuration Release

☑ Zip published projects ⓘ

☑ Add project's folder name to publish path ⓘ

Figure 10.8 – Publish Project

You can explore the other **Advanced**, **Control Options**, and **Output Variables** expanders but the defaults should be fine.

12. Right-click on **Archive Files** and choose **Remove Task**.

You are now ready to publish that artifact to DevOps.

Publishing an artifact

To publish the artifact, follow these steps:

1. Click on **Publish Artifact: Drop** on the left side.

   This is what uploads your newly zipped output folder to DevOps's artifact storage for further release later. The defaults in this section should be fine.

2. Click on the **Triggers** tab. Check the **Enable continuous integration** box, and ensure that **Include** is selected for the master branch. This is what triggers builds on every push to master.

3. Click **Save & queue** under the **Save & queue** dropdown (to the right of the tabs).

4. When the **Run pipeline** dialog box appears, fill in a comment just like you would when committing code, and click **Save** and **Run**.

5. Click on the **Pipelines** tab on the far left, which will bring you back to the list of pipelines.

    The pipeline that you named should show, and the icon should be blue on your screen indicating that it is executing the build pipeline. If it is finished, or after a minute or so, it will turn green.

6. Click on the larger list item to go to the list of the builds for that pipeline, or the text of the commit message to go directly to those build details.

On the **Summary** tab, you should see a variety of information, including the build number, branch, commit, number of artifacts published, and list of jobs. Next to the **Summary** tab may be other tabs. These can be added by other plugins. Clicking on the job indicated by the green check displays the individual steps that the agent used to build your artifact. All standard out (console output) is captured and saved for use in the debugging build errors. Usually, build errors will be prominent and direct you to the location of the error.

Deploying your artifact to Azure

Now that your artifact is built and zipped, we'll deploy it to Azure:

1. Click on the **Releases** subsection under **Pipelines** on the left. Click on **New Release Pipeline**. Once again, a familiar **Select a Template** screen should be shown.

2. You can scroll down or search for **Functions** in the list, select the one that says **Deploy a Function App to Azure Functions**, and click **Apply**.

    You should now see a stage pop out named **Stage one**. This entire section can be customized with different business workflows according to your needs. For this exercise, we will have a single environment.

3. Change the stage name to Production. Click on **Add an Artifact**. Select the source of the artifact, which in our case is a build artifact – which may already be selected.

4. Select your project and then your source build pipeline. Leave the latest as the default version and your source alias should already be pre-populated. Click **Add**.

One of the most powerful opportunities when deploying to Azure is CD. Every time your code is checked in and approved, a version is created and deployed.

Continuous deployment

Your artifact name should now be in the **Artifact** section. Take the following steps:

1. Select the lightning bolt icon on the artifact to show the CD triggers.

2. Enable the CD. This is how we automate the creation of a release after the build is completed.

3. Click on the lightning bolt icon on the production stage. This is also part of the automatic deployment configuration. **After Release** should be selected by default; however, if you do not want the release pipeline to automatically start, then select **Manual Only**.

4. Next, click on the **1 Job, 1 Task** label with the red icon, or you can select the **Tasks** tab. This should look similar to the build pipeline that we created earlier. There should be a few items highlighted in red indicating that they need attention.

5. Select your Azure subscription from that drop-down list. If there is an **Authorize** button, click it.

6. Select **Function App on Linux** for your app type, and then under the **App service name** dropdown, you should see all of the available Linux Azure functions. Please note that if the resource was created recently, it may not show up immediately.

7. Click on **Run On Agent** and use the same agent settings that we did in the build pipeline: **Azure Pipelines** for the agent pool and **ubuntu latest** for the agent specification. The rest of the defaults will be fine.

8. Finally, click on **Deploy Azure Function App**. You can change the display name to something more descriptive if you'd like. Notice that the Azure subscription app type and Azure Functions app name are grayed out. These should match the ones we selected when we selected the production stage.

9. Click on the triple dots under the package or folder label and then navigate down to the artifact ZIP that was built, as shown in *Figure 10.9*.

Figure 10.9 – Select a file or folder

10. For the runtime stack, select **.NET isolated 8.0** and leave **Start with Command** blank.

11. Expand the application and configuration settings and click on the triple dots next to the app settings. This may look familiar to you because this is where we are going to set up the application settings as we did in *Chapter 6*.

12. Click on **Add** and use the same name that we used in Azure before: `MyReturnProperty`. For the value, and keeping with the consistency of what we have seen before, you can use something such as *my value from DevOps*. (If you have spaces in this value, be sure to put it all in double quotes.)

13. Click **Ok.** The name-value pairs should be joined together into a single string in the app settings.

14. Next, click on **Save**, and fill out the comment if you want. You can leave the folder as a slash, or if you know you will have a lot of release pipelines in the future you can organize them into folders here. Then, click **Ok.**

We're not quite done. We must test the release pipeline to ensure that everything works as expected.

Testing the release pipeline

Now, let's test our release pipeline:

1. Click on **Create release** in the upper right-hand corner. You should see the **Create New Release** flyout. You can do temporary one-off adjustments on the manual or automated settings for each of the stages. You may want to create the release, but not necessarily actually push it out to production. You should see the artifact that was created in the build pipeline along with a proper version.

2. Click **Create**. Since we left the stage set to automated, it should automatically begin releasing. Click on the newly created release and you should see a blue in-progress icon, or green if it has already succeeded.

3. You can click on a stage to show logging information under **Summary** along with what commits were made in this new release. Back in the production stage, you can click on logs, which will bring you to the log view of the release pipeline.

> **Note**
>
> For demonstration purposes, disable authorization by going to the authentication section in your function application resource and clicking on the **Edit Text** link (by the **Authentication settings** header). Select **Disable**. Click **Save**. (Be sure to re-enable this when you are finished testing.)

Once the release has finished, navigate to the **Function1** URL we were using in *Chapter 6*, or refresh if it is still open in the browser. It should now display the settings that we configured in the release pipeline: *my value from DevOps*.

End-to-end testing

Let's test to make sure it is all working:

1. Go back to Visual Studio and make a small edit (e.g., a comment).

2. Commit, and then push that to the master branch. Back in DevOps, go to the **Pipelines** section and you should see that that pipeline is already building. Wait for it to complete, then navigate to the release pipeline. You should see that a brand-new release was created immediately after the build succeeded and should now either be running or perhaps even completed already.

Congratulations! You have set up a pipeline that automatically deploys an Azure function HTTP trigger on every commit to the master branch!

Piece of cake!

Summary

In this chapter, we focused on deploying our Azure function using CI/CD.

We saw how to set up the pipeline and connect it to our function. We also saw how to enable deployment to fire every time code is pushed to the master branch.

You try it

Create a simple Azure function. Next, create a new pipeline that automatically deploys that Azure function on every commit to the master branch. Take your time; there are a lot of steps.

Congratulations!

You have worked your way through creating APIs and seen how to migrate your work to Azure. You have conquered many advanced topics and are ready to implement enterprise APIs. Thank you for hanging in there with us, and be sure to let us know what you liked (and didn't!) about this book. Finally, if you have the time, please leave a review on Amazon. You know what they say: if you liked it, tell Amazon; if not, tell us!

In the next and final chapter, we briefly point you to additional resources. We hope they are helpful as you go forward.

11
What's Next?

By this point, you've seen and worked with the fundamentals and advanced topics of creating .NET APIs. The obvious question is, *"What next?"* There are a number of areas where you may want to expand your knowledge and expertise. This chapter will list some of the most important ones.

C#

The #1 place to put your effort is advanced C#. The more you know about C#, the easier it will be to create world-class APIs. Pay particular attention to Linq as much of your retrieval code will make extensive use of it. Even if you don't write in Linq, other API creators will, and you'll need a solid working knowledge of Linq to understand their work.

SQL

The next most important place to put your effort is expanding your SQL skills. The API programmer is, very often, called upon to retrieve the requested data from a database, and in most cases, that will require a working knowledge of SQL.

Note that there are different flavors of SQL depending on what database you are using; however, the core of SQL is the same across platforms.

Database

In addition to expanding your SQL skills, you will want to become as proficient as you can in the database platform you're working with (e.g., Entity Framework). As noted previously, the SQL you'll use will vary a bit depending on which platform you choose (or was chosen for you).

API architecture

There are numerous books that delve into the finer points of architecting APIs. They can be very helpful when designing a very complex API.

Dapper

Dapper is a powerful object relational mapper that we've been using throughout this book. There is more to Dapper than we've needed, however, and it will be valuable to learn some of the more advanced features. You can learn more about Dapper at `https://dappertutorial.net/`.

AutoMapper

We used AutoMapper to map our DTOs to their related **Plain Old C# Objects** (**POCOs**) objects. AutoMapper can map any two objects, which can come in handy in solving more advanced API issues. You can learn more at `https://automapper.org/`.

Visual Studio

Visual Studio is your primary tool for creating APIs, and the more you can learn about it, the easier your life will be. Pay particular attention to creating snippets as they can save you a lot of time. There are a great many features in Visual Studio that we didn't need to go into but are worth learning about. Be sure to become proficient in using Visual Studio to interact with your version control system.

Git

As discussed in the book, while there are other version control systems, the great majority of the C# community (and most other programming languages and platforms) has settled on Git. Becoming proficient in Git in both Visual Studio and at the command line will save you a great deal of time and can prevent panic when you think you've lost your work (you almost certainly have not).

In addition to the numerous tutorials available online, I have a book, *Git For Programmers*, published by Packt, that covers using Git in both the command line and Visual Studio.

Housing your version control

There are three very popular places to house your Git repository:

- On-premises
- On GitHub
- On Azure

On-premises simply means that your Git repository is on your own computer. This can be convenient, but also dangerous. If your repository is on a local computer, damage to that computer can cause your work and work history to be lost.

Microsoft offers two homes for Git. GitHub is popular with open source and smaller applications. For open source applications and small individual users, it is free. The alternative is to put your repository on Azure Repos. Azure DevOps offers a limited free tier, which may suffice for small teams or individual users. It also provides several paid tiers that include additional features tailored for larger projects and more complex team requirements.

Summary

Thank you for sticking with us, and good luck with your work building REST APIs. We know that, armed with this book, you will be successful.

Thank you again,

Jesse Liberty

Joseph Dluzen

Index

packtpub.com

Subscribe to our online digital library for full access to over 7,000 books and videos, as well as industry leading tools to help you plan your personal development and advance your career. For more information, please visit our website.

Why subscribe?

- Spend less time learning and more time coding with practical eBooks and Videos from over 4,000 industry professionals
- Improve your learning with Skill Plans built especially for you
- Get a free eBook or video every month
- Fully searchable for easy access to vital information
- Copy and paste, print, and bookmark content

Did you know that Packt offers eBook versions of every book published, with PDF and ePub files available? You can upgrade to the eBook version at packtpub.com and as a print book customer, you are entitled to a discount on the eBook copy. Get in touch with us at customercare@packtpub.com for more details.

At www.packtpub.com, you can also read a collection of free technical articles, sign up for a range of free newsletters, and receive exclusive discounts and offers on Packt books and eBooks.

Other Books You May Enjoy

If you enjoyed this book, you may be interested in these other books by Packt:

.NET MAUI for C# Developers

Jesse Liberty, Rodrigo Juarez

ISBN: 978-1-83763-169-8

- Explore the fundamentals of creating .NET MAUI apps with Visual Studio
- Understand XAML as the key tool for building your user interface
- Obtain and display data using layout and controls
- Discover the MVVM pattern to create robust apps
- Acquire the skills for storing and retrieving persistent data
- Use unit testing to ensure your app is solid and reliable

Building an API Product

Bruno Pedro

ISBN: 978-1-83763-044-8

- Master each stage of the API lifecycle
- Discover technologies and protocols employed in building an API product
- Understand the different API design definition and validation techniques
- Generate an API server from a machine-readable definition
- Understand how to set up and analyze API monitors
- Familiarize yourself with the different gateways for releasing an API
- Find out how to create an API portal that attracts users
- Gain insights into planning and communicating API retirement to users

Packt is searching for authors like you

If you're interested in becoming an author for Packt, please visit `authors.packtpub.com` and apply today. We have worked with thousands of developers and tech professionals, just like you, to help them share their insight with the global tech community. You can make a general application, apply for a specific hot topic that we are recruiting an author for, or submit your own idea.

Share Your Thoughts

Now you've finished *Programming APIs with C# and .NET*, we'd love to hear your thoughts! Scan the QR code below to go straight to the Amazon review page for this book and share your feedback or leave a review on the site that you purchased it from.

`https://packt.link/r/1835468853`

Your review is important to us and the tech community and will help us make sure we're delivering excellent quality content.

Download a free PDF copy of this book

Thanks for purchasing this book!

Do you like to read on the go but are unable to carry your print books everywhere?

Is your eBook purchase not compatible with the device of your choice?

Don't worry, now with every Packt book you get a DRM-free PDF version of that book at no cost.

Read anywhere, any place, on any device. Search, copy, and paste code from your favorite technical books directly into your application.

The perks don't stop there, you can get exclusive access to discounts, newsletters, and great free content in your inbox daily

Follow these simple steps to get the benefits:

1. Scan the QR code or visit the link below

https://packt.link/free-ebook/978-1-83546-885-2

2. Submit your proof of purchase
3. That's it! We'll send your free PDF and other benefits to your email directly

www.ingramcontent.com/pod-product-compliance
Lightning Source LLC
Chambersburg PA
CBHW080533060326
40690CB00022B/5110